THE SUMMER TABLE

LISA LEMKE

·RECIPES AND MENUS·
FOR CASUAL OUTDOOR
ENTERTAINING

STERLING EPICURE
New York

STERLING EPICURE
New York

An Imprint of Sterling Publishing
1166 Avenue of the Americas
New York, NY 10036

First Sterling edition 2015
This edition has been published by arrangement with Bonnier Fakta

Originally published under the titles Till Sommaren by Lisa Lemke and Till Grillat by Lisa Lemke

ISBN 978-1-4549-0438-0

Distributed in Canada by Sterling Publishing
c/o Canadian Manda Group, 664 Annette Street
Toronto, Ontario, Canada M6S 2C8
Distributed in the United Kingdom by GMC Distribution Services
Castle Place, 166 High Street, Lewes, East Sussex, England BN7 1XU
Distributed in Australia by Capricorn Link (Australia) Pty. Ltd.
P.O. Box 704, Windsor, NSW 2756, Australia

For information about custom editions, special sales, and premium and corporate purchases,
please contact Sterling Special Sales at 800-805-5489 or specialsales@sterlingpublishing.com.

Manufactured in China

2 4 6 8 10 9 7 5 3 1

www.sterlingpublishing.com

Contents

Introduction

I t's summer and you want to hang out and eat well. But how on earth can you choose from all the fantastic things that summer's pantry has to offer and at the same time make everyone happy, satisfied, full, and relaxed? The solution is as simple as it is brilliant: relaxed food that's cooked from the heart and eaten with people you like. If you look abroad, you'll see that that is exactly what *tapas, mezze,* and, say, a six-course family meal in Laos, is all about—connecting with people you care about over a delicious meal. And how can you not love that! I'm from Sweden, and in this book you'll see lots of food and drinks that Swedes love. In my world, I call *all* of this "food for entertaining," because that's exactly what it is all about. Food is meant to be shared.

Easy-to-love dishes are the best for entertaining, whether they come together in a formal dining room, an elaborate buffet, or a battered old picnic table. The most important thing is that we eat together. That is the essence of my food philosophy.

I invite you to summer's absolute best food for entertaining, from simple meals—just for you and someone you like—to dinners for lots of guests. Grilling is a summer delight, so you'll find plenty of reasons in these pages to fire up the grill. At the back of the book you'll find lots of extra side dishes and sweets, because you can never have enough of these special treats.

Food for entertaining my way is easy and beautiful. If you follow my shortcuts, tips, and tricks, when it comes to planning, everything will come together effortlessly, so that you can devote more time to relaxing with your company—and eating well, of course!

Dig in!

Lisa

My Best Tips

My must-haves in the kitchen

There are many things I couldn't do without in the kitchen, especially when it's time to throw a party: a good knife, a laser-sharp grater, a real pepper mill, two large cutting boards, a good mixer or food processor, a large pot, and some small saucepans, to name just a few of the basics. Add in some large bowls, a whisk, spatula, and a bunch of dish towels for drying dishes, gripping hot pots and pans, and, not least, drying off your hands. For me, the most important must-have is good company.

My kitchen suggestions

Freshly ground pepper is always best. Therefore, give yourself two pepper mills as a present, if you don't already have a couple. You're worth it!

When chopped herbs are called for, I like them finely chopped, and I pack them fairly loosely in the measuring cup when I specify amounts.

Fruits and vegetables should always be rinsed and trimmed, with the exception of mushrooms and delicate berries, such as strawberries and raspberries, which I only rinse just before using.

I use real butter, heavy cream, crème fraîche, yogurt, and other high-quality, full-fat products when I cook. But it's up to you to decide what's best for you. Let your heart and stomach guide you.

In several recipes I call for stock or broth. You can use home-cooked stock or canned stock; just don't use the concentrated stuff.

Enjoying a really good cheese once a week is preferable to eating a mediocre one every day. This rule especially applies to cooking. Choose good cheeses, like real feta cheese made from goat and sheep's milk, paired with good wine. Fine meat from healthy animals and good butter are a must (better seldom and good than often and just okay).

Soak white onions, red onions, yellow onions, and shallots in water for a few hours before it's time to peel them—it'll make the job much easier, and might save a tear or two.

Get to know your oven!

Oven temperatures vary, so I have invested in a light analog thermometer that always hangs in the oven, making it easier to control the heat. This is a smart tip, whether you have a new oven or a faithful old one. With only a few exceptions, I specify temperature based on ordinary oven heat, not convection. If you use a convection oven, think about reducing the heat a little bit.

What is "mise en place"?

In the restaurant industry, you can get into a lot of trouble if all the proper mise en place isn't ready before your guests arrive. "Mise en place" simply means that everything you need has been chosen and is ready to go before any cooking actually begins. This is also a smart trick to use in your own kitchen. Gather everything you need and take a moment to consider what can be prepared in advance, before you fire up the stove. For example, all the root vegetables in a recipe can be peeled beforehand and kept in cold water in the refrigerator for at least a day. Above all else, carefully read through a recipe before you start cooking. That way, you won't have any unpleasant surprises, like discovering that you've forgotten the cherries you bought at the market, just when you're getting ready to bake some fantastic cherry squares.

Forget the paper plates!

When throwing a big party, most people don't have enough china. Renting is one alternative. Another is to go for a beautiful vintage table setting with mismatched plates, glasses, and cutlery. You can pick up some real bargains at flea markets, or borrow some dishes and glassware from friends and neighbors. Decorate the table with wildflowers, twigs, and grasses in low glass vases (Just be sure to keep the grasses away from the brother-in-law who has allergies.) Give an extra thought to lighting. If the party will be after sundown, consider use mini light strands—a great way to give outdoor space a cozy feel.

Empty plates or leftovers?

Ask anyone who is throwing a huge buffet party what their biggest nightmare is, and they'll usually say "not enough food." As a result, hosts often overdo it, and there is so much left over that there's no doubt what you'll be eating for the next two weeks. True enough, it is very difficult to estimate food for a lot of people, and there's just no way to know if the minced lamb burgers or the rice salad will be the hit of the party. There are a few tips, though, to keep in the back of your mind, and which should come in handy the next time you plan a big buffet party.

Most people take more food from the first dishes on a buffet table than anywhere else. Therefore, you should place bread, filling salads, and the like, at the beginning of the buffet line. Hopefully, guests will help themselves to large portions of these fillers as they move down the line. Food served as small bites should end up last on the table, where everyone begins to limit their portions a little more, either because of lack of space on the plate or because looking at so much fabulous food has begun to make them feel "full."

When it comes to food for entertaining, it's never a good idea to put dishes together willy-nilly. (Fig marmalade, grilled chorizo, and spicy Asian noodle salad will never be a hit trio.) Give some thought to the composition of the dishes, so that your guests are less inclined to load up their plates with a mishmash of food. Instead, arrange the food as you would a cohesive tasting menu. This will encourage your guests to make two, three, or maybe four trips to the buffet table. You can even leave small signs on the table that explain, for example, which sauce goes with a certain dish; which salad is utterly phenomenal with the marinated meat; and which savory pie absolutely must be eaten together with the pickled vegetables. To make it extra clear, you can also set the table with smaller plates so that guests will be less inclined to simply load food from all the dishes and bowls at the same time.

When you are calculating how much food you'll need for each adult at a meal, it's usually safe to allot approximately 5 ounces of meat, poultry, or fish; approximately 5–7 ounces of prepared pasta, rice, or potatoes; approximately ¼ cup of prepared sauce (this varies a little depending on whether the sauce is thin or thick); and approximately 3½ ounces of raw vegetables. These also are good guidelines for buffets. There are other variables to think about as well: Will the food be served in the middle of the day or later in the evening? People normally eat a little less during the day, compared to the evening. If it is a dinner for both children and adults, then this will influence portion sizes.

A Little Grill Guide

Whether you are in a rush or have a lot of time to prepare the grill for a party or even a simple family gathering, there are plenty of ways to make it a success. More than anything else, it's all about choosing the right ingredients.

If I have a lot of time, I try to choose a whole bird or a large steak that can be cooked for several hours, using indirect grilling. I also like to grill ribs using that method, or I precook them and then grill the ribs for a short time on high heat.

If I'm pressed for time, I choose easier to handle pieces of meat of the highest quality that require only a little salt, pepper, and maybe a glaze. As an extra, I might prepare a little chimichurri as a topping for the meat after it has been grilled.

Different types of vegetables, fish, or perhaps a homemade hamburger made with coarsely ground beef and seasoned with garlic and a little chipotle paste or liquid smoke are also quick and delicious options for the grill. Skewers with cubed meat are a great alternative for the grill master who is short on time. (Just make sure that whatever you put on the skewers requires the same amount of grilling time.) And finally, there's the obvious last-minute choice: sausage. High-quality sausage is, in my opinion, one of the best things you can grill.

Direct and indirect grilling

Direct grilling means that you place the food directly over the hot coals. Because the heat is so strong, direct grilling works best for thinner slices of meat, cutlets, sausage, vegetables, and most fish—and the high heat lowers the risk of the fish sticking to the grill.

Use indirect grilling when you want to cook larger cuts or a whole bird. If you use this method, move the warm coals along the sides of the grill. (To do this, use a heat-resistant rake or spade, preferably steel or aluminum.) The food is then placed in the center of the grill with no coals underneath it. The cover remains closed with the ventilation ports open, which enables the heat to circulate inside the grill. This way, the meat can remain on the grill for a while but stay juicy. It is important to check the temperature from time to time, however, so that it doesn't get too hot. If that happens, you just need to open the cover for a moment or two. If the coals die out before the food is ready, you can always add more coals along the sides of the grill (just be sure to light them in a chimney-starter or a simple steel bucket, before adding them),

Dare to experiment

In order to give your grilled food exciting flavors, you can experiment with different kinds of wood chips, herbs, and twigs from fruit trees (such as apple and plum).

Get the grill going

I suggest lighting the grill early, preferably at least 30 minutes in advance. I use an electric grill lighter, partly for the sake of the environment—not to mention safety—but also because I dislike the taste of lighter fluid in food. Speaking of fire safety, it's always a good idea to have a bucket of water near the grill.

Wait for the coals to glow

For the best results from your grill, wait for the coals to be just right—when they're glistening white and so hot that you can hardly hold your hand over them, even for a few seconds. All too often, we don't wait long enough. We rush and get burned hotdogs or charred burgers. After we've already emptied our plates, alas, the coals are at their best.

Waiting for the grill to be just right is important for other reasons, too—it's the critical time to unwind and discover how hungry you actually are. You're craving . . . what? A special salad, maybe? Or a new take on an old sauce? The waiting moments are when you get great ideas for just the right accompaniments for the perfect steak, fish, sausage, or chicken breast.

Check the temperature

To get the best results from your grill, a cooking thermometer is a smart investment. There are several kinds of thermometers designed just for grilling. I use digital cooking thermometers, either those with a cord that sit in the meat the whole time or the cordless variety that you insert into the meat only when you want to check the temperature. These thermometers read the temperature quickly, and you don't have to fuss with the cord when you're trying to turn the meat. Just be sure to always insert the thermometer into the thickest part of the meat and avoid coming into contact with any bones, because they have a higher temperature than the meat.

People often tell me how stressed they feel when grilling, because "everything happens at once": The potatoes are ready at the same time as the salad and sauce. Just as the guests are arriving, the coals need to be lit. And the fish needs to be ready at the same time as the sausage, ribs, and skewers with mushrooms and onions. And, holy cow, what happened to the drinks?

Relax—everything will work out. It just takes a little planning. For example, have some snacks ready for your guests when they arrive, to take care of the worst hunger pangs. Breadsticks, for example, are perfect for grabbing while the coals are heating to perfection. Sauces and salads can be prepared ahead of time, while the chicken is marinating, and potatoes can always be quickly thrown together. Choose food that, quite simply, can almost take care of itself, so that you can devote yourself to more important things, like keeping an eye on the coals, sipping a blueberry mojito, and nibbling on a few crostini with savory toppings.

With so many options for snacking, try not to go overboard while the grill is being prepared and save plenty of room for the feast! Before the night is over, you will have enjoyed dips of all kinds; salads; filling foods enriched with sauces and butters; and, of course, a whole lot of sweets. And what dinner would be complete without a sweet ending?

~SWEET & SAVORY~ Flavor Boosters

Marinades, Rubs, and Glazes

I deally, you should give some thought to marinades, rubs, and glazes the day before you plan to grill meat, chicken, or fish, in order to give it plenty of time to soak in a marinade for several hours, preferably overnight in the refrigerator. Before you grill, drain off the marinade. Brush on more marinade during the actual grilling—just be sure to let it cook sufficiently (since it has been in contact with raw meat) before you take the food off the grill.

Rubs are a mix of dry spices, and sometimes slightly moist ingredients, such as the zest and juice from lemons and other citrus. Using your hands, thoroughly rub blends into meat, poultry, or fish— and don't be stingy with the rub. Give the meat at least 3 hours to absorb all the flavors of the rub before grilling.

Glazes are brushed onto meat when it is almost done. The purpose of the glaze is to bring out even more flavor from grilled meat and to give each piece a glossy, sumptuous look. In order to give the glaze time to caramelize, brush it thinly onto the meat at intervals. This will give the meat a sticky, intensely flavorful coating.

When it comes to marinades, I love the quartet of soy, apple, ginger, and chile. It goes with everything and works in all situations. I use freshly pressed apple juice because it is a little more tart than concentrate. The ancho chile has a mild heat, so if you want your marinade to pack a bigger punch, you can always use hotter peppers.

Hot Honey and Apple Marinade

About 1¼ cups ✦ 15 minutes

 2 cloves of garlic
 ¾ cup freshly pressed apple juice
 ¼ cup honey
 2 teaspoons finely ground dried ancho chile
 1½ tablespoons finely grated fresh ginger
 ¼ cup plus 3 tablespoons dark soy sauce
 ¼ cup red wine vinegar
 ½ teaspoon coarsely ground black pepper
 ¼ cup apple sauce

Finely chop the garlic and place in a pot together with the remaining ingredients. Bring to a boil and let simmer uncovered on medium heat for 10 minutes.

Let the mixture cool and, optionally, puree it in a blender until smooth. Pour the marinade in an airtight jar or bottle, and keep in the fridge for up to 1 week.

This is one of my absolute favorite marinades. To eat precooked ribs that have soaked in this marinade before grilling is heavenly. But it can be used just as easily to save a mediocre everyday cut of chicken or pork.

Sticky BBQ Marinade

About 1¼ cups ✦ 10 minutes

 2–3 cloves of garlic
 2 teaspoons finely chopped red chile, such as Fresno
 ⅔ cup cherry marmalade or jam
 ¼ cup plus 3 tablespoons hoisin sauce
 ¼ cup plus 3 tablespoons light soy sauce
 2 tablespoons red wine vinegar
 1 teaspoon coarsely ground black pepper

Finely chop the garlic and place it in a pot together with the other ingredients. Bring to a boil and simmer covered for about 5 minutes. Stir now and then.

Let cool, then pour the marinade into an air-tight jar or bottle, and keep in the fridge up to 1 week.

This rub makes me think of North Africa, India, and the Middle East. It's aromatic, hot, and spicy, and it goes especially well with lamb, chicken, and pork.

Quick Spice Rub

About ½ cup ✦ 5 minutes

1½ tablespoons whole coriander seeds
2 teaspoons flake salt
1 teaspoon coarsely ground black pepper
1½ tablespoons mild paprika powder
1 teaspoon ground cardamom
2 teaspoons ground ginger
1 teaspoon cayenne pepper
2 teaspoons brown sugar
2 teaspoons ground cumin

Grind the coriander seeds coarsely in a mortar. Add the rest of the spices and grind together until smooth.

Save in an airtight jar in the pantry, where it will keep for a few months.

The rub should be massaged into meats a few hours before cooking.

This rub, with its blend of fine herbs, has an exciting smoky flavor. It is good with fish, chicken, lamb, or pork. Give smoked salt a try—it really adds something special to rubs like this one.

Herb Rub
with Smoked Salt

About ⅔ cup ✦ 5 minutes

2 tablespoons smoked salt
2 tablespoons dried tarragon
2 tablespoons dried thyme
1 tablespoon dried parsley flakes
⅛ teaspoon garlic powder
2 teaspoons brown sugar
2 teaspoons coarsely ground black pepper

Combine all the ingredients in a bowl and blend together.

Keep in an airtight jar in the pantry, where it will keep for a few months.

Elderflower and lemon are an unbeatable combination both in desserts and on the grill. I use this fresh glaze, especially on whitefish. Don't be stingy with the black peppercorn—it lends good flavor and a nice heat to this delicious glaze. Elderflower syrup can be found online and in specialty grocery stores.

Elderflower and Lemon Glaze

About ¾ cup ♦ 10 minutes

- ½ red chile, such as Fresno, stemmed and seeded
- ¼ cup plus 3 tablespoons freshly pressed apple juice
  Juice and grated zest from 1 lemon
- ¾ cup concentrated elderflower syrup
- ½ teaspoon coarsely ground black pepper

Very thinly slice the chile lengthwise and combine with the other ingredients in a pot. Bring to a boil and let simmer uncovered on medium heat for 3–5 minutes. Stir now and then. Set to the side and cool.

Pour the mixture into an air-tight jar or bottle and keep it in the fridge up to 2 weeks.

The fact that mustard and pork are a match made in heaven is nothing new, but this sweet and spicy mustard glaze is great even on chicken and beef. Be sure to let the liquid cool a bit before you pour it over the mustard seeds. Heating the mustard seeds too much can give the glaze a bitter flavor.

Mustard Glaze

About ¾ cup   ✦   15 minutes

¼   cup light corn syrup
¼   cup red wine vinegar
¼   cup coarse-grain prepared mustard,
      spicy or sweet
 2   tablespoons yellow mustard seeds
¼   teaspoon Tabasco sauce (or to taste)

Bring the syrup, vinegar, and prepared mustard to a boil in a pot and let the liquid cool for a bit. Place the mustard seeds in a mortar, then pour a little of the liquid over the seeds and grind them coarsely into a paste. Stir the ground seeds into the rest of the liquid in the pot and season with Tabasco sauce.

   Stir the mixture carefully, pour it into an airtight jar or bottle, and keep it in the fridge for up to 2 weeks.

This is a fresh, quickly prepared marinade that makes the sun shine even on the darkest days. It is insanely good with chicken, shellfish, or fish. It also pairs well with pork.

Spicy Peaches

About 1¼ cups ✦ 5 minutes

2	cloves of garlic
1	can of peach halves in syrup (8½ ounces)
1–2	teaspoons chile paste
2	teaspoons Worcestershire sauce
	Juice and grated zest from 1 lemon
1	tablespoon Dijon mustard
2	tablespoons dark soy sauce
½	teaspoon coarsely ground black pepper

Coarsely chop the garlic. In a blender, puree all of the ingredients into a smooth marinade.

Pour the marinade into an airtight jar or bottle and keep it in the fridge, where it will stay fresh for about 1 week.

Sauces

Warm Sauces
Rosemary and Lemon Hollandaise

Roasted Pepper Cream

Homemade BBQ Sauce

Gorgonzola and Green Peppercorn Sauce

Cold Sauces
Bean Cream with Truffle

Curry and Peach Chutney

Mayonnaise with Garlic and Chives

Chimichurri

Pea and Mint Hummus

Quick Yogurt Sauces
Apple Tzatziki

Avocado and Feta Cheese Cream

Béarnaise with Yogurt

Spicy-Hot Mango Sauce

Mint, Lime, and Chive Sauce

There's a reason why the very thought of beef with béarnaise makes us close our eyes dreamily. Chicken and curry sauce, lamb cutlets and tzatziki, and baked potato and garlic butter all have a similar effect. Some dishes simply require a certain type of sauce or butter. Here you'll find cold and warm sauces, dangerously good butter blends, salsas, and quickly made yogurt sauces that will serve you well throughout the grilling season. Who knows, maybe you'll stumble upon your match made in heaven. At any rate, I know what mine is: ribs and Asian cherry salsa. To that I say, beef with béarnaise—eat your heart out!

Warm Sauces

The warm sauces you'll find here require a little more time in the kitchen than quickly-made yogurt sauces, but they are not at all difficult to make. As long as you use good-quality ingredients and have a little patience, you will soon be showing off your sauce-making skills. For red wine sauces, I always use the same high quality wine that I serve with the meal. This makes an enormous difference, believe me. And, for the roasted pepper cream on page 16, you'll want to thoroughly roast the bell peppers to draw out as much flavor as possible. Don't be afraid of the blackened skin. Underneath, you'll discover a fantastic sweetness.

Hollandaise sauce is God's gift to humanity. Here I flavor it with rosemary and lemon.

Rosemary and Lemon Hollandaise

4 portions ◆ 15 minutes

1¾ sticks (14 tablespoons) butter
2 large egg yolks
2 tablespoons water
½ teaspoon freshly squeezed lemon juice
  Grated zest from ½ lemon
1 tablespoon finely chopped rosemary
  Salt

Melt the butter. Fill a large saucepan halfway with water and place a heatproof bowl on top of the pan. Whisk together the egg yolks and water in the bowl. Heat the water in the saucepan, but don't let it start to boil. Constantly whisk the egg batter until it starts to thicken a bit.

Lift the bowl off of the water bath, and while constantly and vigorously whisking, pour in the melted butter in a very thin stream. Be careful not to use the butter's milky-white sediment. Flavor the creamy sauce with lemon juice and zest, rosemary, and salt. Serve right away.

*This flavorful cream goes well with virtually every-
thing on the grill, but is especially good with sausage.
Make a large batch and keep it in the fridge, where it
will stay fresh for about a week.*

Roasted Pepper Cream

4–6 portions ✦ 30 minutes

2 red bell peppers
2 yellow bell peppers
1 large yellow onion
3 cloves of garlic
¼ cup olive oil
Salt and coarsely ground black pepper
½ teaspoon freshly squeezed lemon juice

Preheat the broiler.

Halve, stem, and seed the bell peppers.
Cut the onion in large wedges and
coarsely crush the garlic. Place the
peppers, skin side up, in an oven-
safe pan together with the garlic
and onion. Drizzle olive oil over the
vegetables, toss to coat, and broil
for about 20 minutes or until the
peppers are black and bubbling.

Let the peppers cool completely
and then pull off the skins. Transfer
the peppers and everything in the pan
(garlic, onion, and oil) to a blender or
food processor and puree until smooth.
Season with salt, pepper, and lemon juice
and serve at room temperature.

Making your own BBQ sauce is quick and incredibly good. Sometimes I just pulse the ingredients in a food processor to give the sauce a little more texture. Liquid smoke has a powerful favor, so all you need is a very small amount to give the sauce a wonderfully smoky flavor. You can find liquid smoke in any well-stocked grocery store.

Homemade BBQ Sauce

6 portions ◆ 15 minutes

3 large tomatoes
1 large yellow onion
2 cloves of garlic
1 red pepper, stemmed and seeded
¼ cup olive oil
2 tablespoons Worcestershire sauce
½ teaspoon liquid smoke
3 tablespoons dark brown sugar
2 tablespoons tomato paste
  Salt and coarsely ground black pepper
  Hot sauce, such as Tabasco

Coarsely chop the tomatoes, onion, garlic, and red pepper. Heat a pot with the olive oil and fry the chopped vegetables for a few minutes on high heat. Add all the other ingredients except the salt and pepper and hot sauce and let it cook covered on medium heat for 10 minutes. Stir occasionally.

Blend the sauce with a hand blender (or use a food processor) and season with hot sauce, salt, and pepper. Serve warm or at room temperature.

This is the perfect sauce for those nights when you're on the hunt for something a little creamier, a little bolder, and a little smoother than the usual. If you cook the sauce until it has just simmered all you have to do, before serving, is to warm it up and stir in the Gorgonzola.

Gorgonzola and Green Peppercorn Sauce

4 portions ✦ 10 minutes

2 shallots
1 teaspoon green peppercorns in brine, drained
2 tablespoons butter
2 tablespoons cognac or calvados
¾ cup heavy cream
3½ ounces gorgonzola
Salt

Very finely chop the shallots and green peppercorns. Melt the butter in a saucepan over medium heat, and cook the shallots and peppercorns until softened. Add the cognac and cream and bring everything to a boil. Lower the heat and simmer for about 5 minutes, stirring occasionally.

Remove the pot from the heat and stir in the pieces of Gorgonzola until they've melted. Stir and season with salt.

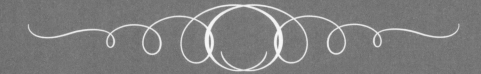

Cold Sauces

Cold sauces are a snap to make. Sometimes, when the sun has burned bright all day and the night air is so warm and filled with the music of crickets that you never want to go back inside, cold sauces fit the bill perfectly. On those evenings, I set out bowls with chimichurri and maybe pea and mint hummus with bread for spreading or dipping, or as a sauce to serve on the side with meat or fish. In the unlikely event that anything is left over, it'll keep for a day or two.

I love quick sauces and dips that can be used for almost anything—as a dip for bread and crackers, a topping for fish, or a dressing for salad. This is that kind of dip. It is so good that I sometimes even lick the bowl. Be sure to add the truffle oil, just at the end and a little at a time, tasting as you go, so that it doesn't becomes too much or not enough of a good thing.

Bean Cream with Truffle

4 portions ✦ 5 minutes

1 can of large white beans
(about 14 ounces)
1 large clove of garlic
¾ cup crème fraîche or sour cream
Truffle oil, to taste
Salt and black pepper

Rinse the beans and pour them in a bowl. Finely chop the garlic and add it to the bowl with a dollop of crème fraîche.

Blend everything into a smooth cream with a hand mixer (or food processor). Add the rest of the crème fraîche and stir. Flavor with truffle oil, salt, and pepper. Keep in the fridge until serving time.

The fruitiness and moderate heat of this chutney is crazy good with grilled pork or chicken. If you want a slightly hotter chutney, choose a curry powder with more bite.

Curry and Peach Chutney

4 portions ✦ 15 minutes

1 large yellow onion
1 tablespoon canola oil
1 tablespoon curry
1 teaspoon turmeric
SCANT ½ cup white wine vinegar
6 canned peach halves in syrup, drained, and syrup reserved
SCANT ½ cup sugar syrup from the canned peaches
Salt and coarsely ground black pepper

Peel and cut the onion into thin rings. Heat the oil in a saucepan over medium heat and sauté the onions, curry, and turmeric for a few minutes. Add the vinegar and cook, covered, for 2–3 minutes, until the onion rings are soft.

Roughly chop the peaches and add them with the sugar syrup in the pot. Cook gently on low heat, covered, for 10 minutes, stirring occasionally. Season the chutney with salt and pepper and pour it into a clean jar. The chutney will keep for about 10 days in the fridge.

I blend all mayonnaise-like sauces with a hand mixer to minimize the risk that the sauce will break or, in other words, become loose, runny, and quite hopeless. But if you're strong, it works just as well to vigorously beat the sauce with a whisk. Some people claim that this makes the sauce even better. Regardless, this sauce goes especially well with fish, preferably a slightly fatty fish.

Mayonnaise with Garlic and Chives

4 portions ✦ 10 minutes

1 large egg in the shell
1 tablespoon white vinegar
1 teaspoon Dijon mustard
1 clove of garlic
¾ cup canola oil
2 tablespoons finely chopped chives
Salt and coarsely ground black pepper

Place the egg in boiling water and let it boil for 3 minutes. Remove it from the heat and rinse it with cold water. Spoon the egg out of the shell and mash it with the vinegar and mustard in a clean bowl. Grate the garlic clove into the bowl and blend everything together with a hand mixer or beat vigorously with a whisk. The mixture can also be pureed in a blender.

While whisking, add a few drops of oil until combined, and then add it in a thin stream while you whisk or blend. Whisk the entire time, until the mixture comes together into a creamy sauce. Flavor with chives, salt, and pepper.

The heat in this Argentinian sauce is determined by how much chile you use. Chimichurri can be poured on grilled beef or pork (delicious!), but it tastes just as lovely with chicken, a good chorizo, and even grilled fish.

Chimichurri

4 portions ✦ **5 minutes**

2	cloves of garlic
¾	cup loosely packed fresh oregano leaves
½	red chile, such as Fresno or fresh cayenne (if it's too mild, you can increase the amount)
SCANT ½	cup good olive oil
2	tablespoons good red wine vinegar
½	teaspoon granulated sugar
	Salt and coarsely ground black pepper

Very finely chop the garlic and oregano. Remove the seeds from the chile and finely chop it. Combine the garlic, oregano, and chile in a bowl and add the oil, vinegar, and sugar. Combine thoroughly and season with salt and pepper. The chimichurri will keep in an airtight jar in the fridge for about 1 week.

This combination of peas and mint always makes me happy. I think it's because of the color. Or the flavors. Or maybe simply because it is so crazy simple and quick to throw together. At any rate, it's fantastic—on grilled bread or chicken, or with a piece of whitefish.

Pea and Mint Hummus

4 portions ✦ 5 minutes

2 heaping cups thawed green peas
¼ cup olive oil
2 sprigs of mint
Grated zest from ½ lemon
1 teaspoon freshly squeezed lemon juice
Salt and coarsely ground black pepper

Mix the peas, oil, mint (use the stems as well if they are tender, otherwise just pull off the leaves), lemon zest, and lemon juice in a food processor or with a hand mixer until smooth. Season with salt and black pepper.

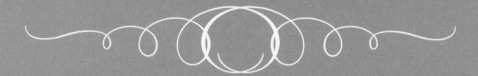

Quick Yogurt Sauces

If I'm in a pinch, a yogurt sauce saves the day. I always have a container of thick Turkish or Greek yogurt in my fridge: On one day it may be transformed into a sauce, in a matter of seconds; on the next day, it may be used to tenderize chicken in a yogurt marinade. The day after that, it might end up on top of a summer cake or turn into dessert instead of the ice cream I forgot to buy (I just add walnuts and fine honey). Here I share my five favorite quick yogurt sauces. But I'm sure you can think of many more, just by looking in your fridge, pantry, or garden.

Yes, this is a tzatziki made with apples instead of cucumbers. It's so easy and so delicious!

Apple Tzatziki

4 portions ◆ **5 minutes**

2 green apples
   Juice from ½ lemon
½ green chile, such as jalapeño or serrano,
   seeds removed
¾ cup whole milk Greek yogurt
2 thick cloves of garlic, pressed or grated
   Flaked sea salt and coarsely ground
   black pepper

Core and grate the apples coarsely. If the apples are particularly juicy, squeeze the grated apples with your hands to drain some of the liquid. Place the grated apples in a bowl and squeeze the lemon juice over it. Finely chop the chile and add it together with the yogurt into the bowl. Add the garlic and stir everything together. Season with salt and pepper. Pour into an airtight container and keep in the fridge.

This creamy, pretty, pale green mix adds a bit of tang as a sauce, dip, or spread, wherever it's needed.

This is my take on a Béarnaise. It's somewhat friendlier to the waistline and is ready before you can say "broken butter sauce."

Avocado and Feta Cheese Cream

4 portion ◆ 5 minutes

1 ripe avocado
3½ ounces feta cheese
1 teaspoon freshly squeezed lemon juice
¾ cup whole milk Greek yogurt
   Coarsely ground black pepper
   Salt (optional)

Peel, pit, and coarsely chop the avocado and place it in a bowl. Crumble the feta into the bowl and add the lemon juice along with a little of the yogurt. Mix everything together into a smooth sauce with a hand mixer or puree it in a food processor. Add the rest of the yogurt. Season with pepper and, optionally, salt.

Béarnaise with Yogurt

4 portions ◆ 5 minutes

4 tablespoons butter, melted and cooled
1 tablespoon dried tarragon
½ teaspoon Dijon mustard
1 teaspoon red wine vinegar
½ teaspoon Worcestershire sauce
⅔ cup whole milk Greek yogurt, room temperature
   Hot sauce, such as Tabasco (a few drops)
   Salt and coarsely ground black pepper

Place the butter and tarragon in a bowl. Whisk together the mustard, vinegar, Worcestershire sauce, and yogurt in a separate bowl. Whisk in the melted butter in a thin stream. Whisk vigorously until well combined. Season with Tabasco sauce, salt, and pepper.

I buy mangoes for this sauce from the freezer section at the supermarket, when they are not in season, so I can make it whenever I like.

Spicy-Hot Mango Sauce

4 portions ✦ 5 minutes

7 ounces frozen mango pieces, thawed
1 tablespoon honey
½ teaspoon chile paste
1½ teaspoons curry
1½ teaspoons tomato paste
⅔ cup whole milk Greek yogurt
1 tablespoon mayonnaise
Salt and coarsely ground black pepper

Combine the mango, honey, chile paste, curry, tomato paste, and a little of the yogurt in the bowl of a food processor. Blend the mixture into a smooth sauce and add the mayonnaise and the rest of the yogurt. Combine everything and season with salt and black pepper.

This is perhaps my most versatile yogurt sauce— use it as a dip, spread, or topping on just about anything.

Mint, Lime, and Chive Sauce

4 portion ✦ 5 minutes

1 clove of garlic
SCANT ½ cup chopped chives
SCANT ½ cup chopped mint
Grated zest and juice from ½ lime
¾ cup whole milk Greek yogurt
Salt and coarsely ground black pepper

Finely chop the garlic and combine it in a bowl with the chives, mint, lime juice, and lime zest, along with a little of the yogurt. Mix everything into a smooth sauce with a hand mixer or in a food processor. Stir in the rest of the yogurt. Season with salt and pepper.

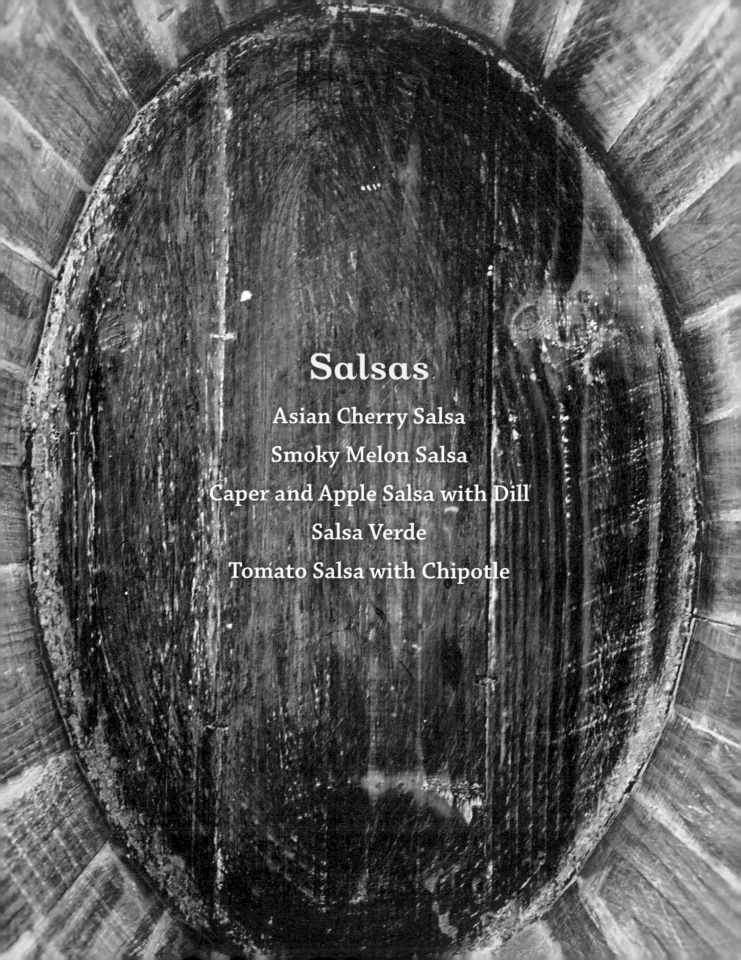

Salsas

Asian Cherry Salsa

Smoky Melon Salsa

Caper and Apple Salsa with Dill

Salsa Verde

Tomato Salsa with Chipotle

Let's salsa! What actually is a salsa? Besides a passionate dance, I mean. These amazing toppings and accompaniments can be anything you want them to be. I like to have a little tartness in my salsas, but I'm not so picky about fine chopping—it's enough to just chop. I go with my feelings. One day the salsa is fine; the next it's rough. Sometimes it's a little runny; sometimes it has the consistency of a chopped salad. Just go with your gut and feel the rhythm.

This salsa is outstanding, especially when you serve it with ribs that have been slathered in Sticky BBQ Marinade (see page 4). The cherries should be lightly mashed to bring out their fantastic flavor. If you can, wait a bit before fishing out the cherry pits, so they have time to give the salsa a little extra flavor.

Asian Cherry Salsa

4–6 portions ✦ 10 minutes + 1 hour

1–2 cloves of garlic
2 tablespoons finely grated ginger
1½ tablespoons rice wine vinegar
1½ tablespoons light soy sauce
1 teaspoon ground star anise
Pinch granulated sugar
1 pound fresh cherries
Coarsely ground black pepper
Salt (optional)

Finely chop the garlic and combine with the ginger, vinegar, soy sauce, star anise, and sugar in a bowl. Stir until the sugar has dissolved. Add the cherries and crush them gently with a mortar so that they are lightly mashed and the flavor blends into the other ingredients. You can also squeeze the mixture by hand if you don't have a mortar. Season with black pepper and, optionally, a little salt. Pour the salsa into a jar, secure the lid, and let it cool in the fridge for at least 1 hour. Be sure to remove the pits from the salsa before serving.

Liquid smoke in a bottle is as magical as a genie in a lantern. I use it often as a flavoring in hamburgers or marinades, and it's incredibly good with watermelon. But go easy on the stuff, even a tiny amount gives a lot of flavor.

Smoky Melon Salsa

4 portions ✦ 5 + 20 minutes

1 pound seedless watermelon without the rind

1 small red onion

¼ teaspoon liquid smoke

½ teaspoon smoky hot sauce, such as Chipotle Tabasco

1 tablespoon canola oil

¾ cup coarsely chopped cilantro
Flaked sea salt and coarsely ground black pepper

Cut the watermelon into cubes and place them in a bowl. Thinly slice the onion and add it along with the liquid smoke, hot sauce, canola oil, and cilantro. Combine everything and season with salt and pepper. Refrigerate the salsa for 20 minutes before serving.

The first time I made this salsa, I served it with grilled mackerel and the combination of the sweet and salty salsa and the fatty fish was heavenly. Try it with grilled cod, salmon, or any other fatty fish.

Caper and Apple Salsa with Dill

4–6 portions ✦ 5 minutes

1 large apple, like Granny Smith
3½ ounces (about ½ cup) whole or coarsely chopped capers (small)
¾ cup chopped chives
¼ cup chopped dill
2 tablespoons olive oil
Coarsely ground black pepper

Core the apple and dice it into small cubes. Combine the apple cubes with the capers, chives, dill, and oil in a bowl. Season with coarsely ground black pepper.

You're probably thinking, salsa verde, isn't that a sauce with parsley, anchovies, capers, garlic, and olive oil? Yeah, but here comes a variation on that theme. With a vibrant flavor and wonderful tartness, this take on salsa verde goes perfectly with grilled whitefish, chicken, or veal. If you like, you can cut the ingredients into larger pieces for a chunkier salad, but here I prefer them finely chopped with heaps of cilantro. If you don't like cilantro, you can use parsley instead.

Salsa Verde

4 portions ◆ 10 + 20 minutes

1 tart green apple, such as Granny Smith
Grated zest from 1 lime
Juice from ½ lime
1 avocado
⅓–½ green chile, such as jalapeño or serrano, seeded (the amount depends on the desired strength)
2 stalks of celery
¼ cup chopped chives
¼ cup chopped cilantro
1 tablespoon canola oil
Flaked sea salt and coarsely ground black pepper

Core the apple and cut it into ⅓-inch cubes. Place in a bowl and combine with the lime zest and juice. Remove the pit from the avocado and scoop out the flesh. Cut the avocado in ⅓-inch cubes and fold them into the bowl. Finely chop the chile, and cut the celery stalks one or two times lengthwise (depending on the thickness) and then into small cubes. Stir everything together with the chives, cilantro, and oil.

Combine thoroughly and season with salt and pepper. Let the salsa sit for about 20 minutes before serving.

Canned chipotles, which you can find just about anywhere, are smoked jalapeños packed in spicy adobo sauce, and they go perfectly with grilled dishes. You can use the sauce directly from the can or, for more punch, puree whole smoked peppers and use the puree to season sauces and salsas. I just want to warn you about one thing, though: this salsa is really addictive! To make it, I combine canned chipotles with fresh tomatoes, a little honey, and a touch of orange— scrumptious!

Tomato Salsa with Chipotle

4 portions ✦ 5 minutes

14 ounces small tomatoes
½ red onion
1 large clove of garlic
½ teaspoon adobo sauce from canned chipotles
1 teaspoon honey
1 tablespoon freshly squeezed orange juice
¾ cup coarsely chopped parsley
Flaked sea salt and coarsely ground black pepper

Finely chop the tomatoes and thinly slice the red onion and put them in a bowl. Grate the garlic and stir it into the tomatoes with the chipotle sauce, honey, and orange juice. Add the parsley and toss everything together. Season with salt and pepper.

Herb Butters

Truffle and Pine Nut Butter

Garlic and Lemon Butter

Basil Butter

Saffron and Bell Pepper Butter

Chorizo Butter

My best tip for making a good herb butter is simple: use real butter! Few things in the world take on flavors better than butter. Here I invite you to try one of my absolute favorites: a wonderfully green basil butter with a flavor that screams "take me to Italy!" The luxurious truffle and pine nut butter and the garlic and lemon butter are inspired by my friend Marcus, king of garlic bread, who knows that you can't be stingy with the garlic. A piece of advice when it comes to the saffron and bell pepper butter: let the chopped pepper rest on a paper towel before you work it into the butter, otherwise it will release too much liquid. Last but not least, don't miss my chorizo butter—it's really good.

I like flavored butters with a little crunch, so I usually chop the pine nuts so that the butter still contains some small pieces. Just be careful when toasting the nuts, because the line between just right and burned is a thin one.

Truffle and Pine Nut Butter

About 6 portions
5 minutes + 2 hours

¼ cup pine nuts
1¼ stick (10 tablespoons) room temperature butter
1 teaspoon truffle oil
   Flaked sea salt and coarsely ground black pepper

Toast the pine nuts in a medium-hot dry pan until they are golden brown. Make sure they don't burn! Remove from the pan and cool completely.

Finely chop the toasted pine nuts and combine them with the butter and truffle oil in a bowl and season with salt and pepper. Scoop the flavored butter onto a sheet of parchment paper and roll it tightly into a sausage shape.

Freeze the butter for at least 2 hours. Let it sit at room temperature for about 15 minutes before cutting and serving.

Although garlic butter and bread are a natural, this combo of garlic and lemon goes beautifully with steamed or grilled veggies, too.

Garlic and Lemon Butter

About 6 portions
5 minutes + 2 hours

3–4 cloves of garlic
1¼ sticks (10 tablespoons) room temperature butter
   Grated zest from 1 large lemon
1 teaspoon freshly squeezed lemon juice
   Flaked sea salt and coarsely ground black pepper

Finely grate the garlic and combine it with the butter, lemon zest, and lemon juice; season with salt and pepper to taste. Scoop the flavored butter onto a sheet of parchment paper and roll it tightly into a sausage shape.

Freeze the butter for at least 2 hours. Let it sit at room temperature for about 15 minutes before cutting and serving the butter.

Fresh basil doesn't keep forever, it's true, but when the leaves aren't quite fresh enough for a salad, you can make them into a delicious butter that tastes great on just about everything.

Basil Butter

About 6 portions
5 minutes + 2 hours

1 large clove of garlic
¾ cup chopped basil
1 teaspoon good quality olive oil
1¼ sticks (10 tablespoons) room temperature butter
   Flaked sea salt and coarsely ground black pepper

Grate the garlic into a food processor. Add the basil and oil, and pulse until combined. Add the butter, mix together until combined, and season with salt and pepper. Scoop the flavored butter onto a parchment paper sheet and roll it tightly into a sausage shape.

Freeze the butter for at least 2 hours. Let it sit at room temperature for about 15 minutes before cutting and serving.

Saffron is an expensive spice, but a little goes a long way, and this fabulous butter will transform anything into a party dish with just a few minutes of work.

Spicy sausage and smoky pimentón in a butter? It's an amazing combination.

Saffron and Bell Pepper Butter

About 6 portions ◆ 5 minutes + 2 hours

1 red bell pepper
Large pinch (about ¼ teaspoon) saffron threads
Salt
1¼ sticks (10 tablespoons) room temperature butter
1 teaspoon chile flakes
Flaked sea salt and coarsely ground black pepper

Stem, seed, and finely chop the red pepper, then spread it out onto a paper towel and let it drain for a few minutes. Crush the saffron with a mortar and a little salt and transfer it to a small bowl. Add the red pepper, butter, and chile flakes, season with salt and pepper, and stir until combined. Scoop the flavored butter onto a parchment paper sheet and roll it tightly into a sausage shape.

Freeze for at least 2 hours. Let the butter stand at room temperature for about 15 minutes before cutting and serving it.

Chorizo Butter

About 6 portions ◆ 10 minutes + 2 hours

4 ounces chorizo, preferably fresh
1¼ sticks (10 tablespoons) room temperature butter plus 1 tablespoon for sautéing the sausage
1½ teaspoons pimentón (smoked paprika powder)
Flaked sea salt and coarsely ground black pepper

Remove the casing from the chorizo and put the sausage into a small skillet with a pat of butter. Cook over medium-low heat, breaking it up with a wooden spoon, until it is completely cooked through and falls apart. If using dried chorizo, remove the casing and very finely chop the sausage before sautéing it in a little butter. Stir in the pimentón and let cool.

Mix the butter and the cool chorizo together in a bowl and season with salt and pepper. Scoop out flavored butter onto a parchment paper sheet and roll it tightly into a sausage shape.

Freeze the butter for at least 2 hours. Let it sit at room temperature for about 15 minutes before cutting and serving it.

THE MENUS

Mexican Grill Party

Salsa Fresca

The Best Guacamole

Tacos el Vaquero

Whole-Grilled Chipotle Chicken

Grilled Mexican Corn
with Mozzarella and Cilantro

Bean Salad with Rice

Hot Tomato Salsa

Fisherman Tacos with Grilled Salmon

Oven-Baked Stone Fruit
with Coconut and Dulce de Leche

Nothing says "summer" better than the smell of a lit grill! In my opinion, one of the best ways to socialize during the summer months, when you get that hankering for sizzling meat, sausage, and veggies, is to throw a grill party. Life gets a little simpler and calmer when food is cooked over glowing coals. The cuisine that most often inspires me when it's time to fire up the grill is Mexican food. I love slow-grilled meat that is so tender it falls apart if you wave a fork over it, as well as spicy salsas and dips that are easy to prepare while the meat is on the grill. Add warm bread, cooling lime, aromatic cilantro, and hot chiles. It's all so simple and tastes so good!

What a difference summer tomatoes make, especially in a salsa! Made from sweet, plump, red summer tomatoes, this salsa is always delicious.

Salsa Fresca

4 portions ✦ **About 30 minutes**

2	large tomatoes
1	small white onion
SCANT ½	cup cilantro leaves
1	large clove of garlic
⅓–½	chile, such as jalapeño or serrano, seeds removed
	Juice of 1 lime
¾	teaspoon salt
	Chopped cilantro as a garnish

Halve and remove the seeds from the tomatoes. Coarsely chop the tomatoes, onion, cilantro, garlic, and chile, and place them all together in a bowl. Add the lime juice and salt and stir it together with a spoon or blend it lightly with an immersion blender.

Let the mixture sit for about 20 minutes. Garnish with cilantro and serve.

Note: A little extra dash of salt usually does the trick in guacamole and salsas.

Is there anyone who doesn't love a really good guacamole? It's a must on tacos, if you ask me, and just as good as salsa for dipping with tortilla chips. Here, I mash one of the avocados and chop the other coarsely to give the guacamole lots of texture.

The Best Guacamole

4 portions ✦ **10 minutes**

1 jalapeño chile, seeds removed
½ tomato
2 ripe avocados
2 teaspoons freshly squeezed lime juice
¾ teaspoon salt
   Chopped cilantro to taste
   Black pepper

Finely chop the chile and remove the seeds from the tomato. Peel and pit the avocados, then mash one of them together with the lime juice and chile in a bowl. Chop the other avocado and tomato coarsely and fold into the bowl along with the salt and cilantro. Season with salt and black pepper.

This is summer grilling at its best. Rub the spices into the pork loin and give them time to be absorbed. Set the pork on the grill and forget it. Well, almost forget it. Without a lot of effort, the meat will be fabulously juicy and tender. While the pork it taking care of itself, you can get busy with something else. Piñata, anyone?

Tacos el Vaquero

4–6 portions ✦ 15 minutes + 2 hours + 2 hours

2¼ pounds whole pork loin with bone

Spice Paste

3 cloves of garlic
¼ cup tomato paste
¼ cup white wine vinegar
1 tablespoon ground cumin
1 tablespoon adobo sauce from canned chipotles
3 finely crushed whole cloves
2 teaspoons salt
1 teaspoon black pepper

For serving

Tortillas
Salsa
Avocado
Cilantro
Scallions
Tomato

For the spice paste, mince the garlic cloves and combine them with the rest of the ingredients. Place the pork loin bone side down in a pan and make deep cuts into the meat. Pat on the spice mixture thoroughly, even into the spaces between the slices. Let the meat rest in the fridge for at least 2 hours.

Prepare a grill with a cover for indirect grilling—that is, a charcoal grill with coals on only one side of the grill, or light only one side of a gas grill. Sear the meat with the flesh side down until it golden and charred. Turn it and place it bone side down on the unheated part of the grill and close the lid.

Grill the loin for about 2 hours, or until it is really tender and completely cooked through (an inner temperature of about 160°F). Don't turn the meat. Allow the bone side to remain on the grill the whole time. The bone side will be a little burned, but the meat itself will be juicy and delicious.

Let the meat rest for about 10 minutes. Cut it into small pieces and place it on a warm serving dish. Serve the meat with tortillas, salsa, and fixings. Avocado, cilantro, scallions, and tomato are a glorious combination.

Note: If you don't have a grill, this recipe works just as well in an oven. First, sear the meat on all sides, in an oiled, hot skillet on the stovetop, until browned. Then cook the meat in the oven at 250°F for 2–3 hours or until it is tender, juicy, and thoroughly cooked.

Grilled whole meats are incredibly rewarding. By setting aside just a little more grill time, you will get astonishingly juicy and tasty results. Here, I tie the chicken legs together and grill the whole bird on an ordinary grill over indirect heat.

Whole-Grilled Chipotle Chicken

4 portions ◆ 3 + 1½ hours

1 whole chicken, 2½–3 pounds

Spice Paste

3 cloves of garlic
1 tablespoon canola oil
2 tablespoons tomato paste
1½ tablespoons dried oregano
2 tablespoons mild paprika powder
1 tablespoon red wine vinegar
1 teaspoon ground cumin
1 teaspoon light brown sugar
1½ teaspoons salt
½ teaspoon black pepper
2 teaspoons water
Chipotle-flavored hot sauce, such as Tabasco

For the spice paste, mince the garlic and combine with the rest of the ingredients, except the Tabasco. Flavor the mixture with Tabasco to taste. Rub the spice mixture around the whole chicken, and try to get as much as possible under the skin. Tie the legs together with cooking twine and let the chicken rest in the fridge for at least 3 hours.

Prepare a grill with a cover for indirect grilling—that is, a charcoal grill with coals only on the sides of the grill, or light only one side of a gas grill. Place the chicken on the indirect heat side of the glowing coals and close the lid. Grill the bird, turning occasionally and taking off the cover if the chicken gets too brown, for 70–80 minutes, or until it is completely cooked through.

Rip the grilled chicken into small pieces and let people make their own tortillas or tacos.

Note: If you have a real kettle barbeque, you can give beer-can chicken a try. You simply stick a half-filled beer can inside the cavity of the chicken and set it upright on the grill so that it looks as if the chicken is sitting on the beer can. Keep the grill covered on indirect heat for 70–80 minutes. Open the lid occasionally to make sure that the chicken doesn't burn.

This combo of grilled corn, mozzarella, and cilantro is guaranteed to be the hit of the party, especially if you can get your hands on super fresh corn from your local farm, CSA, or farmers market. It is amazingly good!

Grilled Mexican Corn with **Mozzarella** and **Cilantro**

4 portions ✦ 1 hour + 30 minutes

Marinade

2	cloves of garlic
2	tablespoon tomato paste
4	teaspoons adobo sauce from canned chipotles
½	stick melted butter
1	teaspoon ground cumin
2	teaspoons honey
4	fresh ears of corn with husks
	Salt and black pepper
4½	ounces (about 1 cup) grated mozzarella
1	sprig of coarsely chopped cilantro
	Finely chopped jalapeño chile (optional)
	Cooking twine
	Aluminum foil

For the marinade, mince or crush the garlic and combine with the rest of the ingredients.

Pull back the husks on each ear of corn without tearing them off completely and tie them together with cooking twine. This will be a useful handle when eating the corn. Trim the cobs, brush off any silk, and brush a thick layer of the marinade on each cob. Place the corn in a plastic bag and let it marinate for about an hour.

Prepare a hot fire in a charcoal grill or preheat a gas grill to high heat. Remove the corn from the bag, season each cob with salt and pepper, and wrap each cob in aluminum foil. This will make four grill packets with the husks sticking out.

Place the packets on the grill over hot coals with the husks sticking out of the edge of the grill so they don't burn. Close the lid and grill the corn for 15–20 minutes or until the corn feels soft when you prick it with a toothpick. Turn the packets halfway through the grilling time. If the corn is really fresh, a shorter grilling time may be enough, and if it's a little older, it may need a little more time on the grill.

Open the packets and top with grated mozzarella, cilantro, and, optionally, chile. Serve immediately.

If you want your tortillas to be a little hardier, try this phenomenal bean salad. You can prepare it a few hours in advance and then spoon it into your tortilla before you top it with other good things.

Given the dizzying array of chiles that is available these days, there's something for everyone, whether you're a tough guy who can take the heat . . . or not. Either way, this salsa is delicious.

Bean Salad with Rice

4–6 portions   ✦   35 minutes

2   cans of various beans 14 ounces each
     (e.g., pinto beans and black beans)
1   small can of corn (8.75 ounces)
2½ cups cooked long grain rice
6   scallions
2   cloves of garlic
2   large tomatoes
2   avocados
     Grated zest of 2 limes (preferably organic)
4   tablespoons freshly squeezed lime juice
     Salt and black pepper

Rinse the beans and corn thoroughly and combine with the rice in a bowl. Slice the scallions and chop the garlic and tomatoes. Peel and pit the avocados and coarsely chop the flesh. Stir everything into the bowl with the rice. Add the lime zest and juice and combine everything thoroughly. Season with salt and pepper.

Let stand for about 30 minutes.

Hot Tomato Salsa

About 4 portions   ✦   About 30 minutes

3   tomatoes
1   small yellow onion with skin
2   cloves of garlic with skin
1   jalapeño chile
1   teaspoon freshly squeezed lime juice
     Salt

Grill the tomatoes, onions, and garlic over hot coals for about 20 minutes, turning the veggies every few minutes or so, until the skin is almost black and the onion feels soft. Place the chile on the grill for the last 5 minutes. Let everything cool.

Peel the onions and garlic and place them in a food processor bowl. Peel the tomatoes, core and remove the seeds, and add to the onions.

Remove the seeds from the chile and any skin that has blackened. Add the chile and lime juice to the processor and blend until smooth. Season with salt.

This fish is very simple to grill—just place the salmon skin side down on a really hot grill, and it will take care of itself. A special grill rack or a fine-mesh grill net is a good investment, however. Either one will do a great job of keeping fish from breaking, crumbling, and falling through the grill.

Fisherman Tacos with Grilled Salmon

4 portions ✦ 40 minutes

Marinade

5	bay leaves
¼	cup vegetable oil
	Juice and grated zest of 1 lime (preferably organic)
SCANT ½	cup chopped cilantro
2	finely chopped cloves of garlic
1½	teaspoons ground cumin
½	teaspoon cayenne pepper
1	pound side of salmon with the skin
	Salt and black pepper

Mango Salsa

9	ounces fresh or frozen mango pieces, thawed
1½	tomatoes
ABOUT ½	jalapeño chile, seeds removed
¼	cup chopped cilantro
	Grated zest from 1 lime
1½	tablespoons lime juice
	Salt and black pepper

For Serving

	Taco shells
1	small red onion, sliced
	Cilantro leaves
	Lime wedges

For the marinade, finely crumble or crush the bay leaves in a mortar. Combine them with the rest of the ingredients in a small bowl.

Place the salmon in a baking dish and rub the marinade on the flesh side. Cover with plastic wrap and let rest in the fridge for no longer than 20 minutes.

Meanwhile, make the mango salsa. If the mango pieces are large, chop them into ½-inch cubes and put them in a bowl. Remove the seeds from the tomatoes with a spoon and thinly slice them along with the chile. Stir everything into the bowl together with the cilantro, lime zest, and lime juice. Season with salt and black pepper.

Prepare a hot fire in a charcoal grill or preheat a gas grill to high. Season the salmon with salt and black pepper and grill with the skin side down over hot coals for 7–9 minutes or until the fish is cooked through and flakes when you poke it with a fork. Serve the salmon in taco shells with the mango salsa, sliced red onion, and cilantro along with the lime wedges on the side.

When I invite lots of people to dinner, I prefer to spend my time at the grill, so that I can socialize with my friends while tending the coals. And to limit the amount of time I spend in the kitchen making dessert, after my guests have arrived, I do as much prep as possible beforehand. This dessert recipe, for example, can easily be assembled in advance. All I have to do is put the pan in the oven about a half hour before it's time for dessert. After that, it goes straight to the table and everyone digs in!

Oven-Baked Stone Fruit with Coconut and Dulce de Leche

6 portions ✦ 2–3 hours

4 fresh pears
2 fresh nectarines
6 soft plums
⅔ cup cane sugar
Juice and grated zest of 3 limes (preferably organic)
2 tablespoons butter

For Serving
⅔ cup shredded, unsweetened coconut
1 can (14 ounces) unsweetened condensed milk for Dulce de leche (see recipe on page 244)

To make the Dulce de Leche, set the can of unsweetened condensed milk in a large pot and completely cover with water. Bring the water to a boil, lower the heat, and let it simmer for 2–3 hours, covered. (See page 244 for more details.)

To prepare the fruit, preheat the oven to 400°F. Halve the nectarines and remove the stones. Place the halves sliced-side up in a baking dish or roasting pan.

In a mortar, grind together the cane sugar, lime zest, and lime juice. Evenly sprinkle the lime sugar over the fruit, particularly in the space left by the removed stones. Shave butter over the fruit and place in the middle of the oven. Bake the fruit for 20–25 minutes or until the fruit is soft.

Meanwhile, toast the coconut. Heat a dry frying pan on low heat and pour in the coconut. Toast while stirring until the coconut becomes golden brown. Watch out, this part happens quickly!

Top the oven-baked fruit with toasted coconut and serve together with the dulce de leche.

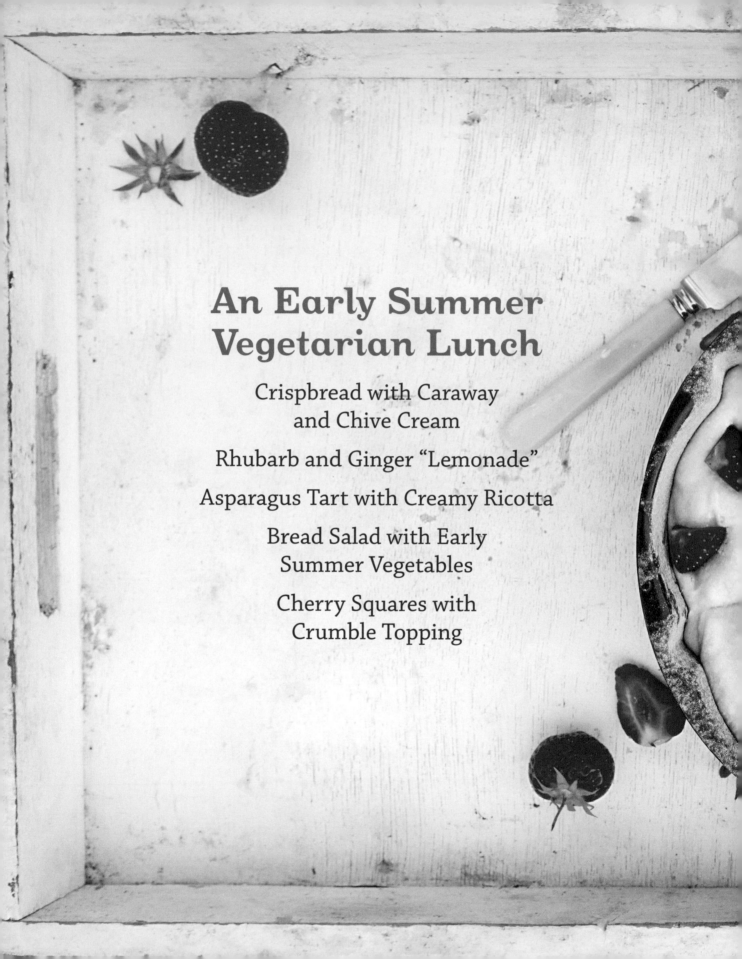

An Early Summer Vegetarian Lunch

Crispbread with Caraway
and Chive Cream

Rhubarb and Ginger "Lemonade"

Asparagus Tart with Creamy Ricotta

Bread Salad with Early
Summer Vegetables

Cherry Squares with
Crumble Topping

As soon as it is just warm enough to sit outdoors, tender rhubarb and Bing cherries start to show up at the market. Sometimes I combine them in a single luscious dessert, but here you can savor them in a few different combos. A rhubarb and ginger pairing, for example, makes a festive and refreshing lemonade-style drink to go with the chive and yogurt crispbread, and the cherries end the meal in a delicious little crumble. Bread salad makes the most of summer's earliest and prettiest veggies. It's really all you need to go with the asparagus pie. I tend to serve it separately though, and why not? It extends the meal and takes center stage . . . until the cherry squares steal the show.

Crispbread with Caraway and Chive Cream

4 portions ◆ 5 minutes + 3 hours

¾ cup whole milk Greek yogurt
2 teaspoons caraway seeds
SCANT ½ cup finely chopped chives
Salt
Crispbread for serving

Pour the yogurt in a fine-mesh strainer lined with a coffee filter or a clean kitchen towel and let it drain over a bowl for about 3 hours.

Finely crush the caraway seeds in a mortar and combine with the drained yogurt and chives in a bowl. Season with salt and allow to marinate for at least 30 minutes.

Serve on crispbread.

You can whip up this recipe for a refreshing rhubarb and ginger "lemonade" as fast as you can drink it—and without all of the elbow grease it takes to make regular fresh lemonade. Serve this fantastic drink ice-cold.

Rhubarb and Ginger "Lemonade"

6 cups ✦ **About 25 minutes**

7	ounces rhubarb (about 2 stalks)
2	inch piece fresh ginger
SCANT ½	cup granulated sugar
6	cups water
	Ice

Peel and slice the rhubarb and ginger into thin slices. Place everything in a nonreactive saucepan (not aluminum) together with the sugar and water. Bring to a boil and let simmer, covered, for about 10 minutes. Remove from the heat and let cool for 10–15 minutes before straining the liquid.

Pour the mixture into a pitcher with a generous amount of ice—or, preferably, a large cube of ice that won't melt and water down the drink too quickly.

If there's any juice left over, an excellent way to save it is to pour it into a clean bottle and keep in the fridge for a few days. You can even freeze it in clean recycled plastic bottles—just don't fill them all the way up because the liquid will expand as it freezes.

We Swedes love our savory tarts. I'll never forget the time, however, when I mistakenly used lard instead of butter to make some dough. Then there was the time when the butter in a crust had clearly spoiled, and my dinner guests diplomatically suggested that perhaps the dough had a little too much baking soda in it? As penance for such unfortunate mistakes, I devoted a whole day just to experimenting with dough—and the result? Yes, it became the scrumptious recipe below!

Asparagus Tart with Creamy Ricotta

4–6 portions ✦ 1 hour + 50 minutes

Tart Dough

5	tablespoons cold butter
¾	cup all-purpose flour
SCANT ½	cup whole wheat flour
5	tablespoons (2½ ounces) small-curd cottage cheese
½	teaspoon salt
1½	teaspoons cold water

Filling

2–3	cloves of garlic
9	ounces (about 1 cup) ricotta
¼	cup cooked and squeezed dry baby spinach
SCANT ½	cup finely chopped fresh parsley
⅔	cup grated aged cheese, like Parmesan or Pecorino
	Salt and black pepper
½	bunch green asparagus
3–4	large eggs

Cut the butter into cubes. Quickly work together the butter, flours, cottage cheese, and salt, either in a food processor or by hand in a bowl, until pea-sized clumps form. Add the water and work together quickly into a smooth dough. Wrap in plastic and cool in the fridge for 20 minutes.

Place the dough on a lightly floured work surface and roll out into a disk about ⅛-inch thick.

Add more flour to the surface as you roll so that the dough doesn't stick. Line a 9-inch tart pan or springform pan with the dough. Be sure to press the dough gently along the bottom edge and pinch a little at the top of the side edges. Cut away the excess pie dough that may be hanging over the sides. Cover the pie shell with plastic wrap and let it cool in the fridge for 30 minutes. Preheat the oven to 400°F.

Remove the pie shell from the fridge, remove the plastic wrap, and prick the bottom with a fork. Cover the edges with aluminum foil and prebake in the middle of the oven for about 15 minutes or until the bottom is baked through and begins to brown. Remove the crust from the oven and remove the aluminum foil.

Chop the garlic cloves for the filling and place in a bowl. Add the ricotta and blend together with the garlic, spinach, parsley, and ⅔ of the grated cheese. Season with salt and pepper and distribute the filling evenly in the pie shell. Break off the tough parts of the asparagus. Spread the asparagus lengthwise over the ricotta mixture and lightly press it into the mixture. Crack the eggs over the filling, season with salt and pepper, and top with the rest of the grated cheese.

Bake in the middle of the oven for about 25 minutes, until the eggs are set and the edges are golden brown.

Ah, beloved bread salad! It's filling, crispy, and so easy to make. Here is my variation with early summer vegetables, but you can make it later in the year with your favorite seasonal veggies.

Bread Salad with Early Summer Vegetables

4–6 portions ✦ 20 + 20 minutes

4 thick slices of day-old country-style white bread
2 tablespoons olive oil
2 small grated garlic cloves
1 small head of broccoli
8 asparagus stalks
10 cherry tomatoes
3½ ounces snap peas
1 small red onion
1 4-inch piece of cucumber
1 bunch of pea shoots
1 tablespoon white balsamic vinegar
2 tablespoons good extra-virgin olive oil
Flaked sea salt and coarsely ground black pepper

Preheat the broiler. Bring a large saucepan of salted water to a boil.

Place the bread slices on a baking sheet. Combine 2 tablespoons olive oil and garlic in a little bowl and brush the bread with the garlic oil on both sides. Toast the bread in the middle of the oven, turning frequently, until lightly browned, about 10 minutes total. Let the bread cool briefly and then cut or tear it into rough pieces.

Break the broccoli into small florets. Remove any woody asparagus stems and cut the rest into smallish pieces. Blanch the broccoli and asparagus for about 2 minutes in the boiling water. The vegetables should still be somewhat firm. Rinse in ice-cold water. Halve the tomatoes and snap peas and thinly slice the red onion. Cut the cucumber into bite-sized pieces.

Toss all the cut vegetables with the pea shoots, bread, balsamic vinegar, and extra-virgin olive oil in a serving bowl. Season with salt and pepper and let sit for 20 minutes before serving.

This small, luscious cake with crumble topping (you can skip the crumble if you like) is all you'll need to end the meal. It's such a snap to make you just might want to whip up another one so that you'll have plenty to send home with your guests.

Cherry Squares with Crumble Topping

25–30 pieces ◆ 20 + 30 minutes

Cake Batter

1¾ sticks (14 tablespoons) butter
1¼ cups granulated sugar
4 large eggs
2 cups plus 2 tablespoons all-purpose flour
1 tablespoon vanilla sugar
1 teaspoon baking powder
½ teaspoon salt
14 ounces pitted cherries

Crumble Topping

1¼ sticks (10 tablespoons) cold butter
1½ cups all-purpose flour
SCANT ½ cup packed light brown sugar

Preheat the oven to 400°F. Line a 9 × 13-inch cake pan with parchment paper.

Melt the butter for the cake batter in a large saucepan; cool briefly. Stir in the sugar and then the eggs, one at a time. Combine the dry ingredients in a bowl and fold into the butter mixture. Spread the batter in the lined pan and distribute the cherries evenly over the batter.

For the topping, mix the butter, flour, and brown sugar together with your fingers into a crumbly mixture. Distribute the topping evenly over the cake. Bake in the middle of the oven for about 30 minutes. Let the cake cool and then slice it into squares.

A Getaway Picnic

Carrot and Coconut Soup

Cheddar Biscuits with Roasted Onion

Cherry Cordial

Noodle Salad with Sesame and Lime

Pâté Sandwiches with Asian Coleslaw

Crispy Hoisin Chicken

Oven-Baked Chinese Plums

Creamy Satay Dip with Cucumber Spears

Mango Squares with Coconut Topping

Pack the picnic basket and hop on a bike. Here, I invite you to try a lot of great things, but if you only have time to make the mango squares and a thermos of good coffee that isn't so shabby either. If you decide to be a little more ambitious and put together the makings of a complete picnic, make sure you pack right! The summer heat is fantastic for picnicking—but it can be hard on food. Think about how you'll keep it cool, if you'll be outdoors for a while. Insulated bags are optimal. Ice packs only last so long—so be sure to place them on top of your food and wrap everything in aluminum foil or newspaper for insulation, and to help keep everything cool a little longer. If I don't have any ice packs, I freeze water and juice in plastic bottles. This helps keep everything nicely chilled and supplies refreshing, cold drinks when the bottles thaw in the sun.

Creamy and wonderfully spicy, this soup tastes just as good served warm from a thermos as it does when it is served cold in a bowl. Try swapping out the carrots with sweet potato or pumpkin.

Carrot and Coconut Soup

4 portions ✦ About 20 minutes

1⅓ pounds carrots
2 yellow onions
2 large cloves of garlic
½ chile, such as jalapeño or serrano, seeds removed
1 tablespoon vegetable oil
1½ teaspoons ground coriander
2½ cups chicken stock
1⅔ cups coconut milk
Grated zest of one lemon (preferably organic)
2½ tablespoons freshly squeezed lemon juice
Salt and black pepper

Peel the carrots and cut them into small pieces. Chop the onion, garlic, and chile. Quickly heat a large saucepan with the oil over medium-high heat. Add the onion, garlic, chile, and coriander and cook until softened. Add the carrot pieces and cook briefly, constantly stirring, then add the chicken stock and coconut milk. Bring to a boil and let simmer, covered, for 10–12 minutes or until the carrots are soft.

Working carefully in small batches, puree the soup in a blender until smooth. Flavor the soup with lemon zest and juice, and season with salt and black pepper.

You would be wise to make a double batch of these impossible-to-resist little biscuits, because they'll be gone the minute they hit the table. And don't forget to crumble them over the carrot and coconut soup on page 79. It's so good!

Cheddar Biscuits with Roasted Onion

About 44 little biscuits ✦ **20 minutes + 1 hour**

1⅔ cups all-purpose flour
2 teaspoons baking powder
1 teaspoon salt
⅔ cup prepared crispy fried onions, such as FRENCH'S®
7 tablespoons cold butter
⅓ cup heavy cream
4 ounces (about 1 cup) grated cheddar cheese

Preheat the oven to 400°F. Combine the flour, baking powder, salt, and onion in a food processor. Cut the butter into cubes, add it together with the cream and cheese and pulse until the dough comes together and is smooth. Roll tablespoon-size balls of the dough and place them on a baking sheet lined with parchment paper.

Bake in the middle of the oven until the balls are light golden brown, 12–15 minutes. Remove the baking sheet from the oven and lower the temperature to 200°F. Let the biscuits cool a little, then split them horizontally with a fork and put them back in the oven to toast until they feel dry—this takes about an hour. Store the biscuits in an airtight container.

If you don't have a juicer, you can achieve the same results with cheesecloth or a clean kitchen towel (one that you will still love even with a few stains), a deep bowl, a big rubber band, and a strainer— piece of cake!

Cherry Cordial

About 5 cups of concentrated syrup ✦ **About 20 minutes + 1 hour**

2½ organic lemons
2½ cups rinsed cherries, pitted
1 quart of water
2½ cups granulated sugar
½ teaspoon jam and jelly pectin (can omit if the syrup is frozen and only kept for a short time in the fridge after thawing)

Wash and cut the lemons into slices. In a large saucepan, bring the lemon slices, cherries, and water to a boil and cook, covered, for about 10 minutes. Mash the berries gently with a potato masher or wooden spoon so that all the juice runs out. Remove the pot from the heat and let stand for about 30 minutes.

Line a large fine-mesh strainer set over a bowl with several layers of cheesecloth or a clean kitchen towel. Pour the juice and fruit solids into the strainer, and let it sit and drain for about 30 minutes. Press on the solids with a rubber spatula or twist the towel or cheesecloth tightly to expel as much liquid as possible.

Bring the strained liquid and sugar to a boil in a saucepan. Stir until the sugar has dissolved and remove from the heat. Skim any foam or impurities off the surface of the syrup and stir in the pectin, according to the directions on the package. Pour the syrup into thoroughly cleaned bottles, preferably sterilized. Keep the syrup refrigerated.

To serve, mix as much syrup as you like, depending on how strong and sweet you like your cordial, in a tall glass of cold water.

The bright flavors of some dishes can fade when they're cold, so it pays off to really push the heat in this noodle salad if you're planning to take it on a picnic and eat it cold. Always remember to taste first before you add more hot sauce!

Noodle Salad with Sesame and Lime

4 portions ✦ About 20 minutes

2	tablespoons sesame seeds
10½	ounces (about 3 medium) carrots
5	ounces (about 1 cup) snap peas
1	6-inch piece leek
8	ounces broccoli
3–4	small garlic cloves
10½	ounces dried egg noodles
2	tablespoons vegetable oil
⅔	cup light soy sauce
1½	tablespoons toasted sesame oil
½	cup sweet chile sauce
1–1½	tablespoons chile paste or other hot sauce
4	tablespoons freshly squeezed lime juice
	Salt

Toast the sesame seeds by stirring in a dry frying pan over medium-low heat.

Peel and very thinly slice the carrots. Cut the snap peas and leek into thin strips and split the broccoli into small florets. Chop the garlic. Cook the egg noodles according to the directions on the packaging and set aside.

Heat the oil in a wok or large frying pan over high heat and stir-fry the garlic and vegetables, stirring constantly, for 1–2 minutes. Stir in all the remaining ingredients except the noodles and sesame seeds and fry them in the wok on high heat for 2–3 minutes.

Add the egg noodles and toss everything thoroughly. Add the sesame seeds and season optionally with salt and more lime juice. Serve the salad warm or cold.

I know. The combination of spicy Asian coleslaw and liver pâté sounds a little strange. But believe me, after the first bite you'll become a convert. To make these sandwiches picnic-friendly, bring the slaw and cucumber in a separate container until it's time to assemble the sandwiches and eat them. You'll love the contrast between the fresh crunchy slaw and the smooth richness of the pâté!

Pâté Sandwiches with Asian Coleslaw

4 portions ✦ About 20 minutes

Asian Coleslaw

- 6 ounces (1 large) carrot
- 6 ounces red cabbage
- 6 ounces white cabbage
- 2 tablespoons freshly squeezed ginger juice (see note below)
- 4 tablespoons freshly squeezed lime juice
- 4 teaspoons fish sauce
- 2 teaspoons sesame oil

Sandwiches

- 1 baguette
- ½ cucumber
- 2–3 scallions
  Liver pâté

Cut the carrot into really thin strips lengthwise, or shave into thin ribbons using a potato peeler. Finely slice the cabbages into strips and combine with the carrot in a bowl.

In a small bowl, whisk the ginger juice, lime juice, and fish sauce together with the sesame oil into a dressing. Pour the dressing over the cabbage salad and toss thoroughly.

Divide the baguette into four pieces and slice open each piece of bread lengthwise. Thinly slice the cucumber and scallions. Spread a generous layer of liver pâté on the bread and place the cucumber, scallions, and cabbage salad on top.

If you want a spicier sandwich, you can top it with a little chopped green or red fresh chile.

Note: To make about 2 tablespoons of fresh ginger juice, simply peel and grate a 3–4-inch piece of raw ginger root. Then press the grated ginger through a fine mesh strainer set over a small bowl.

Chicken thighs are a wonderful picnic food, and don't require anything complicated in the way of utensils or dishes. All you need is a little piece of foil or waxed paper to wrap around the bone end to make this chicken dish into the perfect finger food.

Crispy Hoisin Chicken

4 portions ✦ 2 hours + 55 minutes

Marinade

2 large cloves of garlic

¾ cup hoisin sauce

4 tablespoons light soy sauce

2 teaspoons chile paste or other chile or hot sauce

1 teaspoon freshly ground black pepper

2 teaspoons salt

4 large bone-in chicken thighs

For the marinade, finely chop or grate the garlic and combine with the rest of the ingredients in a bowl. Place the chicken thighs in a heavy food-safe plastic bag, pour in the marinade, tie the bag, and shake it so that the marinade covers all the thighs evenly. Cool in the fridge for at least 2 hours. Turn the bag several times while it's marinating.

Remove the chicken from the fridge while you preheat the oven to 425°F. Place the chicken thighs on a baking sheet and roast them in the middle of the oven for about 35 minutes or until they are cooked all the way through. To crisp the skin, once the chicken is cooked through, switch the oven to the broiler setting and cook until the thighs are golden brown and crispy.

If the chicken is browning too quickly before it's completely cooked, you can cover it with aluminum foil.

Something magical happens when you combine sweet plums, warming spices, a dash of honey, and bake it all in the oven. The effect may not be as momentous as World Peace, but it will come awfully close, especially if you serve these sumptuous plums with Crispy Hoisin Chicken.

Oven-Baked Chinese Plums

4 portions ◆ About 45 minutes

4 ripe sweet red or black plums
2 whole star anise
1 teaspoon fennel seed
4 whole cloves
½ teaspoon ground cinnamon
¼ teaspoon freshly ground black pepper
½ teaspoon red pepper flakes
2 tablespoons fresh apple juice
1 tablespoon honey

Preheat the oven to 400°F. Halve and remove the stones from the plums and place them in a small baking dish. Grind all the spices together in a mortar or spice grinder and sprinkle the mixture evenly over the plums. Drizzle the apple juice and honey over them, and then toss everything together thoroughly.

Bake the plums in the middle of the oven for 35–45 minutes or until they are soft. Serve them warm or cold with the Hoisin Chicken.

Satay dip is not only good on grilled chicken skewers, but it tastes darn good with cool cucumber spears when the summer sun is at its highest.

Creamy Satay Dip with Cucumber Spears

4–6 portions   ✦   About 15 minutes

1   cucumber sliced into spears

Satay Dip
2   ounces (about ⅓ cup) roasted and salted peanuts
1   large clove of garlic
½   red or green chile, seeds removed
1   tablespoon vegetable oil for frying
¾   cup coconut milk
1   tablespoon fish sauce
1   tablespoon granulated sugar
    Juice of ½ lime
    Salt (optional)
    Cucumber spears for serving

Finely grind the peanuts in a food processor. Finely chop the garlic and chile.

Heat the oil in a saucepan over low heat. Add the garlic and chile and fry, stirring for a few minutes. Add the peanuts and continue frying on low heat, stirring until the peanuts are really hot and begin to release their oil. This takes a few minutes. Pour in the coconut milk, fish sauce, and sugar, and bring to a boil while stirring. Let simmer on low heat for 3–5 minutes, stirring now and then.

Remove the pot from the heat and season with lime juice and optionally a little salt. Serve the dip cold with cucumber spears.

Mango should be soft, taste sweet, and bring back memories of lazy days on a tropical island. These easy-to-make, wonderfully sticky mango squares are guaranteed to transport you to your own tropical paradise.

Mango Squares with Coconut Topping

25–30 squares ✦ About 45 minutes

1 pound fresh or frozen mango
2¼ sticks (18 tablespoons) room temperature butter
1¼ cups granulated sugar
4 large eggs
SCANT ½ cup whole milk
3 cups all-purpose flour
1 tablespoon vanilla sugar
4 teaspoons baking powder
½ teaspoon salt

Coconut Topping

⅔ cup cane sugar
SCANT ½ cup light corn syrup
⅔ cup heavy cream
7 ounces (about ¾ cup) flaked coconut
5 tablespoons butter

If you are using frozen mango thaw it on paper towels. While the fruit is thawing, preheat the oven to 350°F. With an electric mixer, whip the butter and sugar in a bowl until soft and smooth. Add one egg at a time, while whisking, and then add the milk. Combine the flour, vanilla sugar, baking powder, and salt and fold that mixture into the batter together with the mango. Fold everything together with a rubber spatula until smooth and thick.

Line a baking pan with high edges, about 10 × 16 inches, with parchment paper and spread the batter evenly in the pan. Bake in the lower third of the oven for about 40 minutes or until the cake is baked through.

Meanwhile, combine all the ingredients for the coconut topping in a pot and cook on low heat while stirring for a few minutes.

Remove the cake and distribute the coconut topping on top of it. Raise the oven temperature to 400°F, set the cake in the lower third of the oven, and bake for an additional 15 minutes or until the coconut topping has turned golden brown.

Let the cake cool and then cut it into squares.

Father's Day Barbecue

Rosemary Breadsticks
with Smoked Salt

Campari-Melon Crush

Grilled New York Strip Steak
with Spice Rub

Red Beet Gratin

Cabbage Salad with
Radishes, Bacon, and Lemon

Strawberry and Grappa Sorbet

Because most dads love grilled steak, here is a simple Father's Day barbecue menu that is sure to please. You can always buy the breadsticks from your local bakery, but working with store-bought pizza dough is so easy, it's no sweat to pamper Dad. To get the best flavor from the steak, be sure to thoroughly rub in the spices, at least a few hours before grilling.

When I'm craving pizza and I'm in a hurry, the neighborhood pizzeria is my best friend. For a few bucks, I usually buy a ball of pizza dough that's big enough to make tons of breadsticks or a large pizza. If I have plenty of time, I make a large batch of my best pizza dough, divide it into smaller balls, and then freeze it in plastic bags. Then all I need to do is grab one from the freezer and let it thaw slowly whenever I get a craving for pizza or bread-sticks. Pizza dough keeps well in the freezer for 2–3 months.

Wherever I am in the world, I always turn to this drink—Campari and blood orange—the best combination of tartness and sweetness. Here, I make it even more delicious with the addition of crushed watermelon.

Rosemary Breadsticks with Smoked Salt

About 40 breadsticks ✦ **30 minutes**

10 ounces pizza dough (see grilled pizza dough recipe on page 173)
4 tablespoons finely chopped rosemary
2 tablespoons smoked salt

Preheat the oven to 425°F.

Knead the dough on a floured work surface. Divide the dough into about 40 pieces and roll them out into approximately ¼-inch-thick sticks. They'll be even better-looking if you twist each one. Finish by sprinkling rosemary and salt on the work surface and rolling the sticks in it.

Place the sticks fairly close together on a baking sheet lined with parchment paper. Bake in the middle of the oven for about 10 minutes, or until they are golden brown and feel dry.

Campari-Melon Crush

4 drinks ✦ **5 minutes**

1⅓ pounds seedless watermelon (without rind)
¾ cup Campari
¾–1¼ cups blood orange juice
Ice

Make sure that all the ingredients are very cold. Cut the melon into large chunks. Mix the melon, Campari, juice, and ice in a blender. Serve immediately in a large glass.

Grilled New York Strip Steak with Spice Rub

4 portions ✦ **2 hours + 15 minutes**

1 recipe Quick Spice Rub (page 7)
1 (20 ounce) New York strip steak, chilled

Season the steak generously on both sides with the spice rub and let the flavors meld for at least 2 hours. Then let the steak sit at room temperature until you've built the fire and let the coals burn down, about 45 minutes.

Grill the steak to desired doneness. The internal temperature will be 135–140°F for medium-rare.

Nothing beats a creamy gratin. Here, I combine red beets, potatoes, and goat cheese—and the result makes my tummy all warm and happy. This dish is also a real feast for the eyes, and goes especially well with grilled meats.

Red Beet Gratin

4–6 portions ✦ **About 1 hour**

Béchamel Sauce

- 4 tablespoons butter
- ⅓ cup all-purpose flour
- 2 cups plus 2 tablespoons whole milk
- ¼ teaspoon grated nutmeg
- Salt and ground white pepper

Gratin

- 14 ounces peeled red beets
- 14 ounces peeled potatoes
- 5 ounces chèvre, crumbled
- 1½ tablespoons chopped fresh rosemary
- 2 teaspoons salt
- ½ teaspoon coarsely ground black pepper
- ½ cup grated hard cheese, such as Parmesan or pecorino

Preheat the oven to 400°F.

Melt the butter for the béchamel sauce in a pot and stir in the flour. Whisk in the milk, a little at a time, and bring to a boil while stirring continuously. Let simmer on really low heat for 3–4 minutes, or until the sauce begins to thicken, stirring occasionally. Season the sauce with nutmeg, salt, and white pepper. Set the pot to the side.

Thinly slice the beets and potatoes. Layer the potatoes, beets, béchamel sauce, crumbled chèvre, and rosemary in a baking dish. Season the layers with salt and pepper. Finish the top later with beets, béchamel sauce, and finally the grated cheese.

Bake in the middle of the oven for about 45 minutes, or until the root vegetables feel soft and the gratin is golden brown. Let the gratin sit for a few minutes before serving.

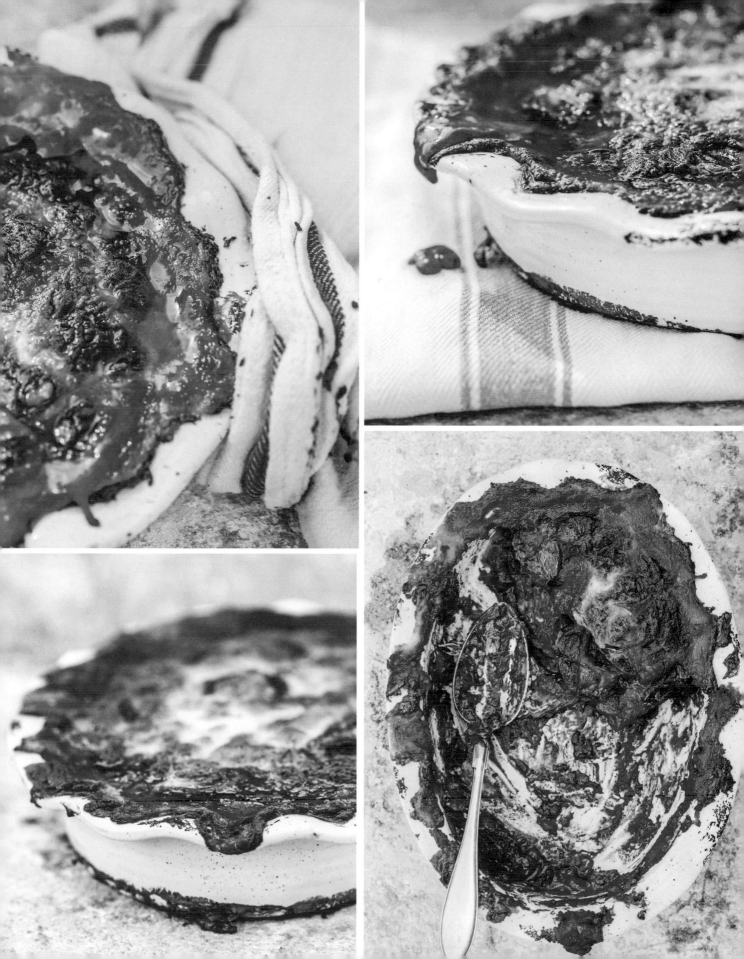

Cabbage is an underappreciated vegetable, which is a shame because there are a number of fantastic varieties. During the summer, when wonderful fresh cabbages are plentiful, I make this simple, finely shredded cabbage salad. This is where the mandoline, one of my favorite kitchen tools, comes in handy. But a sharp knife and a little concentration works just as well.

Cabbage Salad with Radishes, Bacon, and Lemon

4 portions ✦ 10 minutes

5 ounces (about 5 strips) bacon

3 tablespoons olive oil

Grated zest and juice from 1 lemon

Salt and coarsely ground black pepper

½ bunch radishes

1 pound red cabbage

Chop the bacon and fry it until crispy; drain. Stir together the olive oil with the zest and juice from the lemon in a little bowl. Season the dressing with salt and pepper.

Rinse, trim, and very thinly slice the radishes. Finely shred the cabbage and combine with the radishes and dressing in a serving bowl. Season with salt and pepper and top with the crispy fried bacon.

Grappa and strawberries—what a fantastic combination! In this recipe, I use a slightly mild grappa. If you want to make the sorbet even more delicious, use wild strawberries.

Strawberry and Grappa Sorbet

4–6 portions ♦ 15 minutes + 5 ½–6 ½ hours

¼ cup water
⅔ cup granulated sugar
SCANT ½ cup grappa
1 pound of partially frozen strawberries
1 egg white
¼ cup confectioners' sugar

Bring the water and sugar to a boil in a saucepan until the sugar is dissolved. Simmer, covered, for 2 minutes on low heat. Remove from the heat, add the grappa, and let the mixture cool.

Put the cooled syrup and the strawberries into a blender and puree until smooth. Pour the mixture into a shallow airtight container. Freeze for about 1½ hours, or until the mixture is partially frozen.

Whip the egg white and confectioners' sugar together with an electric mixer until fluffy soft peaks form—this takes a few minutes. Loosen the frozen strawberry mixture with a spoon, and fold the meringue into it until no white streaks remain. Smooth the sorbet in the container and freeze for 4–5 hours. Remove the sorbet from the freezer 15 minutes prior to serving.

A Grand Summer Brunch Buffet

Summer Smoothie with Ginger

Baked Eggs with Asparagus and Bacon

Rhubarb and Star Anise Marmalade

Homemade Cream Cheese

Onion, Mushroom, and Sage
Custard Tart

Carrot and Almond Scones

French Toast with a Twist

Summer's Most
Luxurious Granola

There is nothing quite like sleeping in or at least enjoying a lazy start to the day dozing in a hammock or taking a morning dip or an early morning bike ride. But it is also fun, occasionally, to invite your buddies over for breakfast and lunch—or a casual brunch in the shade. Brunch is the perfect excuse to combine everything you like about breakfast and lunch in the same meal.

This smoothie is fresh, delicious, and perfect for a summer brunch. And thanks to the ginger juice, it invigorates your body and soul, as well as your taste buds.

Summer Smoothie with Ginger

4 portions ✦ 5 minutes

10½	ounces half-frozen raspberries and/or blueberries
1–1½	tablespoons fresh or store-bought ginger juice
2–2½	tablespoons honey
2½	cups cold water

Thoroughly blend all the ingredients in a blender or with a hand blender. The drink should be smooth, with the exception of berry seeds.

Serve the smoothie very cold and right away. You can keep it in the fridge for a while, but give it a good stir before serving.

Isn't the egg a truly remarkable thing? Few ingredients are so versatile: You can use eggs in countless recipes, and yet they are perfect all on their own. Having said that, baked eggs—one of the simplest ways to prepare them—are amazingly good.

Baked Eggs with Asparagus and Bacon

8 portions ◆ 20 minutes

Butter for the pan
8 eggs
8 strips cooked bacon
6 green asparagus spears, cut into large pieces
Salt and black pepper
Chile sauce for serving (optional)

Preheat the oven to 400°F. Butter eight cups of a jumbo muffin pan or prepare a baking sheet with large, sturdy paper muffin liners—preferably double-layered so that they're a little more stable.

Crack an egg in every cup and add one slice of bacon. Distribute the asparagus in the cups. Season with salt and pepper and bake in the middle of the oven for 15–17 minutes.

Serve the eggs warm and, preferably, with a good chile sauce.

This is my favorite marmalade—hands down. Rhubarb and star anise are a match made in heaven, and, in my opinion, this marmalade pairs as well with a breakfast sandwich as it does with a wedge of your favorite cheese.

Rhubarb and Star Anise Marmalade

1½–2 cups ✦ 35 minutes

2 whole star anise
1 vanilla bean
1 pound (about 4 stalks) rhubarb
About 1¼ cups granulated sugar

Finely crush the star anise in a mortar or grind it in a spice grinder. Split the vanilla bean lengthwise and scrape out the seeds, reserving the bean. Slice the rhubarb and combine with the star anise and vanilla seeds and bean in a nonreactive saucepan. Bring to a boil and then stir in the sugar. (No additional liquid is required because rhubarb releases its own liquid over high heat.) Reduce the heat and simmer uncovered on medium heat for 25–30 minutes.

Pour the marmalade into a clean, hot jar. (Putting hot food into cold jars can cause them to crack.) When the jar is completely cool, serve the marmalade or cover with a secure lid and store it in the refrigerator and use within a week or two, at the most.

I serve this extremely creamy cheese with only a fine salt or a good marmalade. You can, of course, flavor it to your own liking—horseradish, lemon zest, or chopped herbs are delicious!

Homemade Cream Cheese

About 1 cup
20 minutes + 4–5 hours

3½ cups sour milk
¾ cup heavy cream
Good-quality sea salt

Warm the sour milk and cream in a pot over low heat, stirring until the mixture reaches 130–140°F, or until the mixture curdles.

Pour the mixture into a fine-mesh strainer lined with several layers of cheesecloth, a kitchen towel, or a coffee filter. Let drain for at least 4–5 hours, preferably longer.

Season the cheese with salt and save in a jar in the dairy compartment of the fridge for no longer than 10 days.

This flavorful tart is perfect for baking the day before you serve it. All you need to do is warm it up when it's time for brunch. If you can find them, use seasonal mushrooms.

Onion, Mushroom, and Sage Custard Tart

4–6 portions ◆ About 2 hours

Tart Dough

5	tablespoons cold butter
¾	cup all-purpose flour
SCANT ½	cup whole wheat flour
5	tablespoons small-curd cottage cheese
½	teaspoon salt
½	tablespoon cold water

Filling

3	large yellow onions
2	tablespoons butter
1½	tablespoons granulated sugar
¼	cup good-quality balsamic vinegar
	Salt and pepper
2	ounces mixed wild mushrooms
15–20	sage leaves
3	large eggs
⅓	cup whole milk
⅓	cup heavy cream
¼	cup finely grated Parmesan

Cut the butter for the pie dough into cubes. In a food processor, quickly pulse the flours and butter together until small clumps form (if mixing by hand in a bowl, use a fork). Add the cottage cheese and salt and pulse until combined. Finally, add the water and pulse until the dough comes together. Turn the dough out and knead until smooth. Wrap in plastic and let rest in the fridge for 20 minutes.

Place the dough on a lightly floured work surface, knead it a bit, and roll out into a disk about ⅛-inch thick. If needed, add more flour to the surface so that the dough doesn't stick. Line a 9-inch springform or pie pan with the dough. Be certain to press the dough into the corners of the pan. Cut away any extra pie dough that may be hanging over the sides. Cover the shell with plastic wrap and let it rest in the fridge for about 30 minutes.

Preheat the oven to 400°F. Take the pie shell out of the fridge and remove the plastic wrap. Prick the bottom with a fork, cover the top edges with aluminum foil, and prebake the shell in the middle of the oven for about 15 minutes or until the bottom is baked through and begins to brown. Take the pie shell out of the oven and remove the aluminum foil.

Thinly slice the onion for the filling. Heat a frying pan with the butter and fry the onions until soft without letting them brown. Add the sugar and vinegar and let the liquid boil down. Season with salt and pepper. Chop the mushrooms and sage and stir them together with the eggs, milk, and cream in a bowl. Season with salt and black pepper. Pour the egg custard into the pie shell, distribute the cooked onions over the custard, and top with Parmesan cheese.

Bake the tart in the middle of the oven until the filling has set, about 20 minutes.

As you put together the dough for these amazing scones, you'll probably think, What's going on? I think there's too little flour! But no, the dough should be exactly this sticky. There's nothing to knead or roll here—all you have to do is scoop the dough onto a baking sheet and bake.

Carrot and Almond Scones

About 8 scones ◆ About 15 minutes

½ stick (4 tablespoons) room temperature butter
¾ cup all-purpose flour
¾ cup sifted rye flour
2 teaspoons baking powder
½ teaspoon salt
¾ cup whole milk
4 coarsely grated carrots (about 1⅔ cups)
3½ ounces (about 1 cup) coarsely chopped almonds

Preheat the oven to 425°F. Cut the butter into cubes and combine it with the flours, baking powder, and salt, either in a food processor or by hand until pea-sized clumps form. Add the milk, carrots, and almonds and combine with an electric mixer or stir by hand until combined and sticky.

Scoop eight balls of dough onto a baking sheet lined with parchment paper and bake in the middle of the oven for 10–12 minutes or until golden brown.

Serve with your favorite topping (see recipes for Homemade Cream Cheese and Rhubarb and Star Anise Marmalade on page 113) and enjoy!

This is not French toast as you know it. The combination of bread, pancake batter, and a lot of good berries, makes this version altogether luxurious.

French Toast with a Twist

4 portions ✦ About 30 minutes

¼ cup all-purpose flour
⅔ cup whole milk
1 large egg
½ teaspoon salt
4 thick slices of light bread
 Butter for frying
14 ounces mixed fresh or frozen and thawed berries
 Honey for serving

In a bowl, whisk together the flour and a little of the milk until smooth and clump-free. Whisk in the rest of the milk, egg, and salt until it is a smooth batter. Let the batter sit at room temperature for about 20 minutes.

Scoop out a little bread from the middle of every slice of bread and dip the slices thoroughly in the pancake batter. Heat a frying pan with a generous amount of butter on medium heat and place the bread slices in the pan. Pour a little batter in each hole in the bread slices, along with a few berries, and pour in just a little more batter. Fry the bread slices on both sides until they are golden brown.

Serve the toast warm with the rest of the berries and honey.

Life is too short to eat boring breakfast cereal! Here's a rich granola with lots of good things in it, like dried fruit, crunchy nuts, and a splash of maple syrup.

Summer's Most Luxurious Granola

About 7½ cups ✦ **About 25 minutes**

3 cups rolled oats
¾ cup wheat germ
7 ounces coarsely chopped nuts
¾ cup flaked coconut
SCANT ½ cup whole flaxseeds
¾ cup shelled sunflower seeds
¾ cup pumpkin seeds
½ teaspoon salt
½ cup water
3 tablespoons maple syrup
7 ounces dried mixed fruit

Preheat the oven to 425°F. Combine all the ingredients except the water, maple syrup, and dried fruit in a large sheet pan or roasting pan. Stir together the water and maple syrup and drizzle it evenly over the ingredients. Stir everything until the mixture has formed very small clumps.

Roast the granola in the lower third of the oven for 15–20 minutes or until it feels dry and has begun to turn golden brown. Stir the mixture, now and then, while it is roasting. Chop the dried fruit into small bits and add them to the granola, during the last 5 minutes of cooking time. Let the granola cool and store it in a jar or a bag.

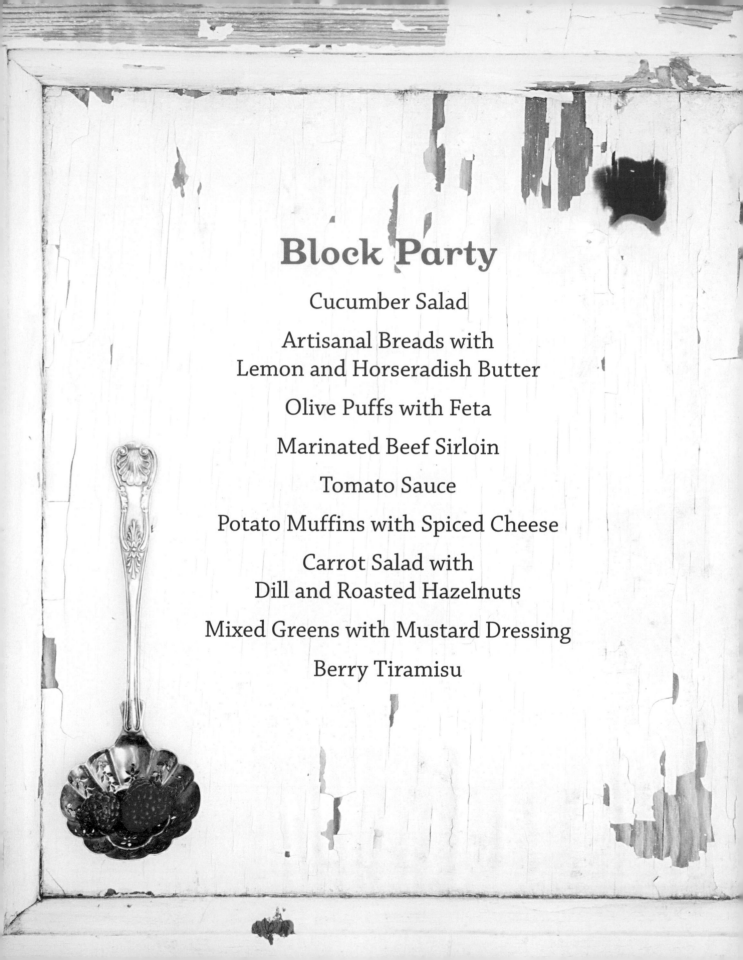

Block Party

Cucumber Salad

Artisanal Breads with
Lemon and Horseradish Butter

Olive Puffs with Feta

Marinated Beef Sirloin

Tomato Sauce

Potato Muffins with Spiced Cheese

Carrot Salad with
Dill and Roasted Hazelnuts

Mixed Greens with Mustard Dressing

Berry Tiramisu

Throwing an amazing party for the whole block requires only a couple of things: recipe and logistical planning (and maybe a bit of luck with the weather). A few weeks in advance, buy drinks and ingredients that keep for a while or can be frozen. Check to make sure that you have all the pots, pans, bowls, plates, glasses, cutlery, tables, and chairs you'll need. One or two days in advance, buy all the fresh ingredients and prepare as many make-ahead dishes as you can. And, if you take a few short cuts, you can easily organize everything you need for a perfect dinner party.

The cucumber, mint, red onion, and lemon in this easy-to-prepare salad make it the perfect choice for an outdoor party or picnic. Keep it cool in the fridge until you're ready to serve it.

Cucumber Salad

About 16 portions ✦ 5 + 20 minutes

1	large cucumber
1½	large red onions
½–1	green chile, such as jalapeño or serrano
⅔	cup chopped mint
	Zest and juice of 1 lemon (preferably organic)
2	teaspoons olive oil
	Salt and black pepper

Cut the cucumber into small cubes. Finely chop the red onion and chile. Combine everything in a bowl along with the mint, lemon juice and zest, and olive oil.

Season with salt and black pepper and let it sit for at least 20 minutes.

Serve with cold smoked salmon or gravlax.

When you're planning a party, you need to focus your attention on something other than baking a lot of bread. Instead, buy really good bread, preferably different kinds, and concentrate your energy on making a wonderful, flavored butter. If you prepare it at least a week in advance—it tastes even better! Just remember to let the butter come to room temperature before you serve it, so it has time to soften.

Artisanal Breads with **Lemon** and **Horseradish Butter**

About 10 portions ✦ 10 + 20 minutes

⅓ cup finely grated fresh horseradish (about

1 ounce unpeeled horseradish)

7 tablespoons room temperature, salted butter

¼ teaspoon black pepper
  Grated zest of 1 lemon (preferably organic)

½ teaspoon fresh lemon juice
  Salt (optional)

Stir all the ingredients together thoroughly in a bowl. Let it sit for at least 20 minutes at room temperature. Season as desired with salt and more horseradish.

Serve with a selection of fresh breads.

If you're a superhero, you can make your own puff pastry. But if you're an ordinary mortal, I think it's totally fine to buy frozen puff pastry. All you have to do is pop them into the oven before your guests arrive.

Olive Puffs with Feta

18 slices ◆ 10 + 20 minutes

2 thawed sheets of puff pastry, 5 × 5 inches
3½ ounces feta cheese made with goat
   or sheep's milk
1 tablespoon olive oil
   Grated zest of 1 lemon (preferably
   organic)
18 pitted kalamata olives
   Salt and black pepper

Preheat the oven to 400°F.

Cut each puff pastry sheet into 1½ x 1½-inch squares. Place the squares, with a little space between them, on a baking sheet lined with parchment paper. Make a small depression in the middle of each square using your thumb. Cut a large piece of the feta cheese and break it into small pieces. Brush all the squares with olive oil and place a piece of cheese into each hollow and top with a little lemon zest. Firmly press an olive into the cheese so that it stays in place during baking when the pastry rises. Crumble the rest of the feta over the squares and season with salt and pepper.

Bake the puffs in the middle of the oven for 15–20 minutes, or until golden brown.

Serve the puffs warm or cold.

Slow-roasted beef sirloin, cut into thin slices and marinated, is magnificent food for entertaining when you're having a lot of company for dinner.

Marinated Beef Sirloin

About 6 portions ✦ **1½ + 3 hours**

1⅔ pounds whole beef sirloin
3 teaspoons salt
1 teaspoon coarsely ground black pepper

Marinade

¼ cup olive oil
½ teaspoon red pepper flakes
Grated zest of 1 lemon (preferably organic)
2 tablespoons freshly squeezed lemon juice
2 large garlic cloves, chopped
SCANT ½ cup chopped fresh herbs, such as oregano, parsley, thyme

Preheat the oven to 300°F.

Salt and pepper the sirloin and rub the spices into the meat thoroughly. Place the meat on a rack set in a roasting pan (so that the liquid from the meat can be collected) and place the pan in the middle of the oven.

Cook for about 1½ hours, or until the meat has reached an inner temperature of 140–150°F. Insert a meat thermometer into the thickest part of the sirloin to check the temperature.

Let the meat rest for 15 minutes and cut it into very thin slices.

In a bowl, combine all the ingredients for the marinade with the pan juice. Place the beef slices in the marinade and let it marinate in the fridge for at least 3 hours. I usually place the beef and marinade in a heavy food-safe plastic bag when it has cooled so that the meat can more easily absorb the marinade.

Serve the sliced meat cold or at room temperature.

Who has time to stand around and chop tomatoes and onions when you need to make dinner for forty people? Exactly. That's where your food processor comes in handy. Let it do all the chopping and pureeing. This recipe for tomato sauce pairs beautifully with beef sirloin.

Tomato Sauce

6 portions ◆ **10 minutes**

1¼ pounds tomatoes
1 large red onion
2 cloves of garlic
1½ tablespoon Worcestershire sauce
1½ tablespoon tomato paste
Herb salt
Hot sauce, such as Tabasco

Coarsely chop the tomatoes, red onion, and garlic and puree them together in a blender or food processor. Pour everything into a saucepan and add the Worcestershire sauce and tomato paste.

Bring the sauce to a boil and let it simmer for about 5 minutes. Stir occasionally. Season with herb salt and Tabasco and serve the sauce either warm or cold.

The sauce can become a little watery if it has been standing for a while. Just warm it up on the stove before you are about to serve it, and it will be perfect again!

Whether you're making simple savory muffins or decadent cupcakes, try using these unique paper liners. In my opinion, most muffin liners are either attractive but not very functional, or functional but not particularly attractive. That's why I make my own liners whenever I bake a pan of muffins. First, I cut out 6 × 6-inch squares from a sheet of parchment paper. Then I press two parchment squares into each muffin cup. I have to say, it looks great.

These muffins are best freshly baked, but if you want to prepare them in advance, you can freeze the muffins as soon as they have cooled. Thaw and warm them before serving.

Potato Muffins with Spiced Cheese

12 muffins   About 30 minutes

1⅔ cup all-purpose flour
1½ teaspoons baking powder
1 teaspoon salt
2 large eggs
SCANT ½ cup natural yogurt or sour cream
SCANT ½ cup water
¼ cup olive oil
3½ ounces coarsely grated firm spiced cheese, such as aged Gouda with cumin, or some other aged firm cheese, like provolone

Filling

6 ounces waxy or russet potato, peeled
Salt and black pepper

Preheat the oven to 400°F. Line a 12-cup muffin pan with paper liners, or set 12 handmade parchment muffin cups on a baking sheet.

Combine all the dry ingredients. Whisk the eggs in a bowl and add the yogurt, water, and oil. Fold the liquid into the flour mixture along with three-fourths of the cheese. Stir until smooth.

Very thinly slice the potato and season the slices with salt and pepper. Fill every liner about three-fourths full with the batter and evenly distribute the potatoes and the rest of the cheese in the muffin cups. Press the potato slices lightly into the batter.

Bake in the middle of the oven for about 20 minutes. These are best served at room temperature—whether freshly baked or reheated.

For a nice variation, try adding chopped dill to the batter—I highly recommended it!

You don't have to go bankrupt to throw a big summer party, when you can use humble ingredients that are easy on the wallet. For example, you can use sweet summer carrots in this salad recipe, instead of asparagus. This way, you can afford to have parties a little more often!

Carrot Salad with Dill and Roasted Hazelnuts

4 portions ✦ 20 minutes

1¾ ounces (about ⅓ cup) hazelnuts
14 ounces carrots
½ stick (4 tablespoons) butter
SCANT ½ cup chopped dill
Flaked sea salt

Toast the hazelnuts in a dry frying pan over medium heat. Let them cool and then coarsely chop them. Peel the carrots and cut them into strips as thin as possible, preferably with the help of a mandoline or potato peeler.

Melt the butter in a saucepan over medium heat, and let it bubble until it is golden brown and begins to have a nutty aroma. Remove the pan from the heat and let it stand for a few minutes. Pour the butter through a fine-mesh strainer to separate the brown residue from the liquid butter.

Drizzle the warm, browned butter over the carrots and top with the hazelnuts, dill, and flaked salt. Serve immediately.

To make this spread extra colorful, buy a couple different kinds of lettuce. Rinse the leaves well in ice-cold water, and then shred them into coarse pieces. Place the greens in a beautiful bowl and serve them with Mustard Dressing—with freshly ground pepper and flaked sea salt on the side.

Mixed Greens with Mustard Dressing

6 portions ✦ 5 + 15 minutes

2 heads of lettuce or a variety of salad greens (different varieties work well), washed and torn into coarse pieces

Dressing
1 tablespoon yellow mustard seeds, ground in a mortar
1 tablespoon whole grain mustard
2 teaspoons white wine vinegar
2 tablespoons heavy cream
  Water
½ teaspoon honey
  Salt and black pepper

Whisk together all the dressing ingredients and dilute with water to the desired consistency. Let the mixture sit for about 15 minutes, so that all the flavors can become integrated, before serving with the salad greens.

Note: Make sure to thoroughly grind the mustard seeds—this works best with a real mortar and a strong pair of hands.

Lovely tiramisu is a crowd pleaser. It is great for entertaining, because it is easy to prep ahead of time, and actually tastes better after a day or two. It is also incredibly easy to dress it up, as I have done in this recipe, with white chocolate, limoncello, and sweet summer berries.

Berry Tiramisu

10–12 portions ✦ 30 minutes + 12 hours

3½ ounces white chocolate

5 large egg yolks

⅔ cup confectioners' sugar

1 pound room temperature mascarpone

SCANT ½ cup water

¼ cup concentrated elderflower syrup

4 tablespoons limoncello (Italian lemon liqueur)

ABOUT 25 ladyfinger cookies

Marinated Berries

ABOUT 2 cups assorted berries (e.g., blueberries, raspberries, and strawberries)

SCANT ½ cup concentrated elderflower syrup

1 tablespoon freshly squeezed lemon juice

Chop the white chocolate and melt it in a bowl over a water bath. While the chocolate is melting, thoroughly whisk the egg yolks and confectioners' sugar in a bowl. Fold in the mascarpone and the cooled melted chocolate and whisk together into an even and fluffy cream.

Cover the bottom of a 9-inch springform pan with a thin layer of mascarpone cream. Combine the water, elderflower syrup, and limoncello in a bowl. Dip about one-quarter of the cookies into the mixture and distribute them evenly over the mascarpone cream. Fill the pan with another layer of cream.

Dip additional cookies in the syrup mixture and add another layer of cookies. Continue to layer the mascarpone cream and dipped cookies until the pan is filled. Cover with plastic wrap and refrigerate for at least 12 hours.

Twenty-five minutes before serving, slice the strawberries and put them in a bowl with the other berries, elderflower syrup, and lemon juice. Let the berries marinate in the elderflower and lemon syrup for 20 minutes.

Gently run a thin, sharp knife around the pan edge, loosen the tiramisu carefully, remove the outer springform ring, and set it on a plate while still on the springform bottom. Drain the berries and then distribute them over the tiramisu just before serving. If there are leftover berries, serve them in a bowl on the side.

Fire Up the Grill for Lunch!

Blueberry Mojito

Grilled Guacamole Tortilla with Mozzarella

Grilled Bass or Mahi Mahi
with Mint, Lime, and Chive Sauce

Summer Risotto with
Asparagus and Basil

Roasted Fruit on the Grill

This menu is all about keeping it simple with foods that can be thrown on the grill and cooked in no time flat. As always, the fish must be super fresh, so buy it on the very day you grill it. You can skip the risotto and simply grill some vegetables if time is tight.

The absolute best mojito I've ever had was at Camps Bay in Cape Town, South Africa. It was made with sun-ripened passion fruit and a lot of love. And that is the secret behind a good mojito—whether it's made with cherries, passion fruit, or only lime. I've made this Swedish summer version with blueberries, and it is so good that time stands still. But watch out for blueberry stains!

Blueberry Mojito

4 drinks ◆ 5 minutes

½ lemon
3½ ounces (about ¾ cup) frozen and lightly thawed blueberries
3 tablespoons raw sugar
1 handful of mint leaves
⅔ cup light rum
¾ cup club soda
Plentiful ice

Slice the lemon in half. Distribute the slices together with the blueberries, sugar, mint, and rum in glasses and muddle so that the flavors are released. Top with club soda and ice. Serve right away.

Is there anyone who can say "no thanks" to guacamole? I certainly can't. Here's my valentine to the dip of all dips—grilled guacamole rolls. Instead of mashing all of the ingredients, I cut them into large pieces so that all the flavors have a chance to pop. These stuffed tortilla are filling, mind-blowingly good, and perfect for the grill.

Grilled Guacamole Tortilla with **Mozzarella**

4 portions ✦ About 20 minutes

2 avocados

1 small red onion

2 tomatoes, preferably different colors

4½ ounces fresh mozzarella

2 cloves of garlic

8 small tortillas

Juice from ½ of a lime

⅔ cup coarsely chopped cilantro

Flaked sea salt and coarsely ground black pepper

Hot sauce, such as Tabasco

Halve the avocados, remove the pits, scoop out the flesh, and cut the flesh into thick slices. Peel and cut the onion into thin rings. Thinly slice the tomatoes. Tear the mozzarella into small pieces and finely chop the garlic. Distribute everything evenly over the surface of the tortillas, squeeze a little lime juice over them, sprinkle some cilantro over each tortilla and season with salt, pepper, and Tabasco. Roll up the tortillas and secure them with toothpicks. Grill the tortillas for about 3 minutes on low heat, preferably over indirect heat, so they're not lying directly over the coals. Turn the rolls halfway through the grilling time. They're ready when they have a little color and the mozzarella has melted. Serve immediately.

This is perhaps my most versatile yogurt sauce, and it's delicious with fish. You can grill any firm whitefish and serve this sauce on the side.

Grilled Bass or Mahi Mahi with Mint, Lime, and Chive Sauce

4 portions ✦ 15 minutes

1 recipe Mint, Lime, and Chive Sauce (page 31)
4 (6 ounce) center-cut pieces striped bass or Mahi Mahi fillet with skin
Olive oil for oiling fish and grill
Salt for seasoning

Make the sauce and set aside.

Prepare a grill for cooking over medium-hot coals. Pat the fish dry and brush it all over with olive oil and season with salt. Oil grill rack and put fish skin side down on grill. Cook, without flipping, for 8–9 minutes for 1-inch-thick fish. Serve with sauce.

Want to know the secret behind a perfectly creamy risotto? Use a wooden spoon and make sure that you stir the risotto often, especially toward the end of the cooking time. This brings out the starch in the rice, which is what makes it so creamy. Stir in the peas and basil just before serving; otherwise, they'll lose their fantastic green color. This risotto is a treat with meat, fish, poultry, and good sausage.

Summer Risotto with Asparagus and Basil

4 portions ✦ About 30 minutes

1	shallot, peeled
1	clove of garlic
1	bunch of green asparagus
1½	tablespoons butter
1¼	cups arborio rice
1⅔	cups dry white wine
3⅓	cups chicken stock
¾	cup frozen green peas, thawed
⅔	cup chopped basil
¾–1¼	cups coarsely grated Parmesan
	Salt and coarsely ground black pepper

Finely chop the shallot and the garlic. If necessary, break off the tough part of the asparagus and cut the rest into ¾-inch pieces, reserving the tips. Heat a large saucepan with the butter and sauté the onion and garlic until soft. Add the rice and let it sauté for a short while. Add the white wine and let the rice boil in it, stirring it now and then. Add a little stock and simmer on low heat. Stir often and add the stock a little at a time until the rice is soft.

Add the asparagus pieces and let them cook while stirring continuously for 2–3 minutes. Coarsely chop the peas and add them, together with the basil and asparagus tips, when the risotto is soft and creamy. Stir in the Parmesan cheese and season with salt and pepper. Serve right away.

Here's a dessert that is insanely easy to prepare. It is also an excellent choice for picnics, but only if you're okay with eating it without ice cream, of course. Lightly whipped cream or a dollop of high-fat natural yogurt with a little confectioners' sugar also goes great with this dessert.

Roasted Fruit on the Grill

4 portions ✦ **10 minutes**

8 sheets of aluminum foil, about 15 × 15 inches

4 cups rinsed fresh berries (e.g. raspberries, blueberries and strawberries)

3½ ounces white chocolate

¼ cup heavy cream
Finely grated zest from 1 lime
Vanilla ice cream, for serving

Double-layer 4 sheets of aluminum foil and distribute the berries over them. Grate the chocolate and spread it evenly over the berries, along with the cream and lime zest. Fold the mixture into 4 packets and tightly pinch the top of the aluminum foil to keep the ingredients from oozing out of the packet. Grill the packets over hot coals for 5 minutes. Serve immediately with vanilla ice cream.

Note: If you put the chocolate in the freezer for about 30 minutes, it's much easier to grate.

Lazy Days
at the Beach Buffet

Iced Earl Grey Tea with Rhubarb

Melon Tricolore with Olives, Basil, and Mint

Veggies with Spiced Yogurt Dip
and Nut and Parsley Crumble

Steak Sandwiches with Horseradish Mayo

Warm Potato Salad
with Pork Belly and Cherries

Bread Omelet with Grapes and Gorgonzola

Summer Salad with Shrimp
and Fall-Over-Backward-Good Dijon Dressing

Strawberry Semifreddo Cones
with Biscotti Streusel

After a long and lazy day on the beach, I know exactly what I want. An ice-cold drink. Fresh and really crisp vegetables. Salty olives. A steak sandwich. Maybe something with a little salty-sweet contrast. And last but not least, ice cream. Loads of ice cream. The perfect end to a great day.

I feel like a kid on Christmas morning when I taste flavors that should clash, but turn out to be scrumptious together, like rhubarb and strong Earl Grey tea. It's delicious as iced tea, and it's a dynamite flavoring for tiramisu as well!

Iced Earl Grey Tea with Rhubarb

4–6 portions ✦ 10 minutes + freezing time

14 ounces (about 4 stalks) rhubarb
¾ cup granulated sugar
1⅔ cups water
3 Earl Grey tea bags
Water for diluting

Slice the rhubarb and put it in a nonreactive saucepan with the sugar, 1⅔ cups water, and tea bags. Cover with a lid, bring to a boil, and let simmer for a few minutes. Remove from the heat and let cool.

Remove the tea bags and pour the liquid through a sieve into a plastic container that has a lid; discard the solids. Freeze, covered, for a few hours. Scrape the ice into a pitcher with cold water until the tea is the desired strength.

Note: Make a huge batch of the tea and freeze it in portions—the perfect refreshment for a hot day.

After a day on the beach, you'll want to revel in cool and delicious delights. My melon salad with salted olives and fresh herbs fits the bill perfectly. You can mix it up with different types of melon, if you like, but it looks and tastes just as good with only one variety.

Melon Tricolore with Olives, Basil, and Mint

6 portions ✦ 10 minutes

2¼ pounds melon (with rind)

7 ounces (about 1¼ cups) kalamata olives with pits

⅔ cup shredded basil

⅔ cup shredded mint

3 tablespoons freshly squeezed lemon juice

3 tablespoons olive oil

Salt and black pepper

Cut the rind from the melon and remove any seeds.

Cut the melon into small pieces (or use a small melon baller) and let them drain for a short while on a tray lined with a clean kitchen towel.

Combine the melon with the rest of the ingredients in a bowl. Serve the salad at room temperature or slightly chilled.

These veggies make the perfect after-beach snack along with something cool in your glass. And I give you permission to double dip—first in the yogurt and then in the crunchy crumble. If you prefer, pour the dip into several small bowls so that everyone gets their own little dip kit!

Veggies with Spiced Yogurt Dip and Nut and Parsley Crumble

8 portions ✦ 20 minutes

Yogurt Dip

1 cup whole milk Greek yogurt
2–3 small cloves of garlic
Grated zest of 2 lemons (preferably organic)
1 tablespoon mild smoked paprika powder
Salt and black pepper

Crumble

1¾ ounces (about ½ cup) whole almonds
1 sprig of parsley
Assorted raw vegetables

Pour the yogurt in a bowl. Add the crushed or minced garlic to the bowl and stir. Mix in the lemon zest and paprika powder. Season with salt and pepper and let the mixture sit for about 15 minutes before serving.

Coarsely chop the almonds and parsley and combine in a bowl. Cut the vegetables into bite-sized pieces, lay them on a plate, and serve together with the dip and crumble.

Note: Smoked paprika, *pimentón de la vera*, is a popular spice in Spain. It is very good and also available in well-stocked grocery stores, specialty shops, and on the Internet.

There's nothing better than a really good steak sandwich. After a day in the sun, when I want something quick and easy to throw together that has a little bite to it, this sandwich is the perfect thing. Horseradish mayo can easily be prepared a few days in advance, but make sure that all the ingredients are room temperature when you're ready to prepare the recipe, in order to keep the mayonnaise from breaking.

Steak Sandwiches with Horseradish Mayo

4 portions ✦ About 20 minutes

Horseradish Mayo

- 1 clove garlic
- 1 room temperature egg yolk
- 1½ teaspoons white wine vinegar
- 1 teaspoon Dijon mustard
- ¼ cup canola oil
- ABOUT ⅓ cup finely grated fresh horseradish
  Salt and freshly ground black pepper

Sandwiches

- ½ baguette
  Sesame seeds
  Red pepper flakes
- 1 red onion
- 1 large tomato
  Butter for frying
- 1 pound piece sirloin steak
  Salt and black pepper
  Finely grated fresh horseradish for topping

Preheat oven to 475°F. To make the mayo, mince or finely chop the garlic and set it in a bowl. Add the egg yolk, vinegar, and mustard and mix together vigorously with an electric mixer or a whisk by hand. While mixing, add a few drops of the oil, and then add the remaining oil in a thin stream, mixing or whisking the whole time, until the mixture becomes a creamy mayonnaise. Stir in the horseradish, season with salt and pepper, and let the mayonnaise sit for about 15 minutes before using it.

Cut the baguette into four equal pieces and split them horizontally. Brush the tops of the bread with water and sprinkle sesame seeds and red pepper flakes over them. Toast the bread in the middle of the oven until golden brown.

Thinly slice the red onion and tomato. Cut the beef into thin slices and pound with a meat mallet until very thin; season with salt and pepper. Heat a frying pan with butter and fry the steak slices on high heat for about 40 seconds on each side.

Assemble the sandwich with all the ingredients and top with the mayo and finely grated horseradish.

Note: Raw meat is easiest to slice thin when it is partially frozen—and the pieces thaw quickly at room temperature.

This warm potato salad is the quintessential summer comfort food:
hearty potatoes, sweet cherries, salted pork, and fresh rosemary.
The best words to describe this dish are "soul satisfying!"

Warm Potato Salad
with Pork Belly and Cherries

4–6 portions ◆ **30 minutes**

1½ pounds small waxy potatoes
2 large yellow onions
1 tablespoon canola oil for the pan,
  plus additional for drizzling
8 ounces salted, smoked pork belly
  Salt and black pepper
10½ ounces (about 2 cups) pitted
  fresh cherries
2–3 sprigs of rosemary
1 bunch of arugula

Preheat the oven to 425°F. Thinly slice the potatoes and the onions and put them in an oven roasting pan with a little oil, tossing to coat the vegetables. Cut the pork into small cubes and scatter it over the potatoes. Season with salt and pepper and drizzle some additional oil over the top.

Roast the mixture in the middle of the oven for 20–25 minutes or until the potatoes are soft and everything is turning golden brown. Add the cherries. Serve the salad at room temperature, with a little arugula on top.

TROT

Fruit in savory food is SO good. It's all about the balance between sweet and salty—think strawberries and goat cheese, dates and bacon, melon and olives. Delicious! The combination of bread, gorgonzola, and grapes in this omelet is outrageously good. Feel free to substitute your favorite type of blue cheese for the gorgonzola. Why not Roquefort?

Bread Omelet
with Grapes and Gorgonzola

6 portions   ✦   About 30 minutes

3–4 thick slices of light sourdough bread

2 tablespoons butter for roasting the bread

6 large eggs

SCANT ½ cup whole milk

¼ cup heavy cream

Salt and black pepper

10½ ounces (about 1¼ cups) whole red or black seedless grapes

7 ounces gorgonzola

2 tablespoons fresh finely chopped thyme

Preheat the broiler.

Cut the bread into rough ¾-inch cubes. Heat an oven-safe frying pan with butter over low heat and toast the bread cubes slowly. While the bread is toasting, whisk together the eggs, milk, and cream and season with salt and pepper.

Place half of the grapes in the frying pan and pour in the omelet batter. (If the bread has soaked up all the butter, you might need to add a dollop of butter to the pan so that the omelet won't stick.) Add the rest of the grapes. Cook the omelet on low heat for about 15 minutes without stirring the eggs. Break the cheese into small pieces and distribute it evenly over the omelet.

Put the frying pan in the oven under the broiler, watching carefully, until the eggs are completely set and the top of the omelet is golden brown.

Garnish with chopped thyme and serve immediately.

Although there is a dizzying array of salad greens at my local grocery store, I usually need to plead with the manager to stock my favorite—frisée. So here's a good tip—nag, pray, and beg long enough and even the busiest greengrocer will eventually give in.

Summer Salad with Shrimp and Fall-Over-Backward-Good Dijon Dressing

4 portions ♦ 15 minutes

Dressing

1	shallot
2	tablespoons heavy cream
1	teaspoon Dijon mustard
1	teaspoon white vinegar
	Salt and black pepper
1	pinch of granulated sugar

Salad

8	ounces cooked, peeled shrimp
5	ounces (about 1½ cups) baby green beans
2½	ounces (about ½ cup) mixed roasted nuts
1	small head frisée lettuce
¾	cup kalamata olives
4	soft boiled eggs
	Flaked sea salt and freshly ground black pepper

To make the dressing, finely chop the shallot and whisk it together with the cream, mustard, and vinegar. Season with salt, pepper, and sugar.

Bring a saucepan of salted water to a boil. Add the green beans and cook until crisp-tender, about 1 minute. Drain and put them in a bowl with the shrimp, nuts, lettuce, and olives and toss well to combine. Drizzle a little dressing over the salad and toss. Slice the eggs in half and distribute them over the salad. Season with salt and pepper and serve right away.

Note: Don't cook the eggs too long; they are better when they're a little creamy.

Semifreddo is the perfect quick ice cream. It is scrumptiously good and easy to make without cooking or using an ice cream machine. Just remember to take the semifreddo out of the freezer about 30 minutes before serving.

Strawberry Semifreddo Cones with Biscotti Streusel

6–8 portions ✦ 20 minutes + 4 hours

9 ounces fresh strawberries (or frozen and almost completely thawed strawberries)
¾ cup sweetened condensed milk
2 large egg whites
¾ cup heavy cream
¼ cup confectioners' sugar
2 large egg yolks
Grated zest and juice from 1 lime (preferably organic)
6–8 sugar cones for ice cream
Crushed biscotti cookies for serving

In a food processor, coarsely pulse the strawberries together with the condensed milk—ideally there should be little bits of fruit in the mixture.

Beat the egg whites into firm peaks in a clean stainless steel bowl and set aside. In another bowl, whip the cream until fluffy. Add the strawberry milk, confectioners' sugar, and egg yolks, along with the lime zest and juice, to the whipped cream and continue to whip until fluffy. Gently fold the egg whites into the cream batter.

Pour the batter into a plastic container with a lid and freeze for at least 4 hours.

Let the semifreddo sit at room temperature for about 30 minutes before serving.

Fill the cones with scoops of semifreddo and top with the crushed biscotti.

An Easy-As-Pie Pizza Party

Grilled Artichokes with Gremolata

Grilled Pizza with Asparagus and Salsiccia

Lisa's Banana Split

I like to think of this menu for a pizza party as an excuse to get together other grown-ups who are kids at heart. Artichokes, cooked on the stovetop in boiling water and then lightly toasted on the grill—are a delicious warm-up for the star of the show—grilled pizza! With a bit of planning, most of the prep for the pizza can be done in the kitchen before your guests arrive, which makes the party a little bit more fun for you as well. And when it comes time for dessert, move the party to the kitchen, where everyone can help make the banana splits.

Grilled artichokes are especially good when they are small and tender. The smaller the artichoke, the shorter the cooking time. To test when the 'chokes are soft enough to eat, insert a sharp knife or skewer into the stalk. If it comes out quickly the artichokes are done.

Grilled Artichokes with Gremolata

4 portions ✦ About 40 minutes

4 tender young artichokes on the stem
½ yellow onion
2 bay leaves
Juice from ½ lemon
1 pinch of granulated sugar
Salt
Olive oil
4 tablespoons butter, for serving

Gremolata

2 cloves of garlic
¼ cup finely chopped parsley
Finely grated zest from 1 lemon
½ teaspoon flaked sea salt
¼ teaspoon coarsely ground black pepper

Prepare a hot charcoal fire in a grill.

Cut away the thick woody portion of the artichoke stems and cut the onion half into wedges. Place the artichokes stem side up in a large pot. Cover with water and add the onion, bay leaves, lemon juice, sugar, and ample salt. Use a cover that's slightly smaller than the pot or a heat-safe plate to keep the artichokes under the water.

Bring the water to a boil, lower the heat, and let the water simmer until the artichokes are soft, about 20 minutes; the time will vary depending on their size. Drain and let the artichokes sit until they are cool enough to handle. Halve them lengthwise and brush the halves with a little olive oil.

Finely chop the garlic for the gremolata and combine it with the parsley, lemon zest, flaked salt, and black pepper in a bowl.

Grill the artichokes over hot coals until they have color on both sides. Serve with gremolata and butter.

Grilled pizza is amazingly good in the summer, for lunch, dinner, or any time, for that matter! The pizza gets a wonderful crispy crust on the bottom and a subtle smoky flavor. Although I usually grill pizza for the main event, I also like to serve it as a hearty appetizer. I have experimented and achieved the best results when I've used a charcoal kettle grill with a round lid, and grilled the pizza on a removable bottom from a springform pan or just a plain old pie pan, if I don't have a pizza pan on hand. A baking stone, of course, works just as well. If you have any avocados at home, put a few thick slices on the pizza before you grill it for a sinfully good treat.

Grilled Pizza with Asparagus and Salsiccia

4 portions ✦ About 30 + 45 minutes

Pizza Dough

4	teaspoons active dry yeast
1	teaspoon honey
1	teaspoon salt
1	cup lukewarm water
2½	tablespoons olive oil
2½	cups all-purpose flour + ¼ cup for baking

Filling

½	bunch of green asparagus
1	red onion
1–2	salsiccia, dried chorizo, or other hard sausage (7 ounces)
3½	ounces chèvre
SCANT ½	cup roasted red pepper relish or pesto
¾	cup coarsely grated Parmesan
	Salt and coarsely ground black pepper

Place the yeast in a bowl. Add the honey, salt, and a little of the water and stir until the yeast has dissolved. Add the rest of the water and the olive oil. Stir in the flour, a little at a time, and work together into a dough. Knead the dough until it smooth and elastic, 5 minutes in a stand mixer with a dough hook or 10 minutes by hand. Let the dough rise for about 45 minutes under a clean towel.

Halve the asparagus lengthwise and finely chop the onion. Cut the sausage and chèvre into thin slices. Turn the dough out onto a floured work surface, divide into 2–4 pieces and knead them lightly until they form a ball. Roll out the pieces into thin pizza crusts and spread red pepper relish over them. Distribute the asparagus, onion, and sausage evenly over the crusts and then sprinkle with chèvre and parmesan. Season with salt and pepper.

Flour a pizza pan and slide the dough onto it. Place the pan on a grill that has hot, glowing coals on the sides. Close the cover and grill for 5–7 minutes or until the pizza is cooked through. Check now and then to make sure that the coals aren't too hot and that the pizza doesn't burn. Bake the other pizzas in the same way.

Is there anything more sweetly nostalgic than a banana split? I think of rockabilly, sundaes, and diners. But the fact is, the roots of this classic dessert go a lot deeper into the past—the banana split has been around for more than a hundred years. Here is my tribute to this venerable old-timer.

Lisa's Banana Split

4 portions ✦ 20 minutes

Chocolate Sauce

3½	ounces good quality dark chocolate (about 70 percent cacao)
1	cup heavy cream
SCANT ½	cup cocoa powder
1	pinch of salt
1	tablespoon butter

Sundaes

4	bananas
SCANT ½	cup raw sugar
4	tablespoons butter
¾	cup finely chopped salted peanuts
	Vanilla ice cream

Coarsely chop the chocolate. Bring the cream to a boil in a medium saucepan, remove the pan from the heat, let cool a little, and then stir in the chocolate, cocoa, and salt. Stir until the chocolate has melted. Add the butter and continue stirring until it has completely melted. Let the chocolate sauce cool briefly.

Split the bananas lengthwise and dip them sliced-side down in the raw sugar so that the cut surface is completely covered with sugar. Melt the butter in a frying pan over high heat and place the bananas sugar side down into the pan. Fry them, without turning, for 1–2 minutes, or until they begin to turn golden brown.

Spread the chopped nuts on a cutting board and carefully set the bananas, fried side down, onto the nuts so that the nuts stick to the caramelized surface.

Serve the just-fried bananas with ice cream and drizzle the warm chocolate sauce over the top. Top with a sprinkle of more nuts, if desired.

Chic Cocktail Party in the City

Bubbly with Raspberry Cognac

Salty-Sweet Rosemary Popcorn

Pizza with Chanterelles, Chorizo, and Pecorino

Cucumber with Miso Dip and Roasted Sesame Seeds

Shrimp with Cilantro and Mint Dip

Rye Slices with Creamy Smoked Sausage Spread

Pane Caramello with Flake Salt

Whative en lazy vacation days are almost over, and everyday life starts to call us back, there is no better thing to do than to drag out the fun as long as possible. Avoid reality for a while and invite your friends to a decadent, smoking-hot cocktail party high above the rooftops.

I'll never forget the first time I tasted a fabulous French raspberry cognac made from the simple combination of cognac and lots of sweet summer raspberries. Here's my own take on this divine drink: I top the whole thing with champagne. It's incredibly good! And, like my mother-in-law says, "A cocktail should have a bit of a kick!"

Bubbly with Raspberry Cognac

6 drinks ✦ 10 minutes

Raspberry Puree

8	ounces (about 2 cups) raspberries
SCANT ½	cup confectioners' sugar

For the Cocktails

¾	cup raspberry puree
4	tablespoons cognac
	Sparkling wine, cava, or dry champagne

Blend the raspberries and confectioners' sugar until liquefied. Pass the puree through a fine-mesh strainer with the help of a wooden spoon or spatula. Keep the puree in the fridge or freezer in small portions so it's ready to use when you need it.

Evenly divide ¾ cup of the cold puree among 6 champagne flutes. Add 2 teaspoons of cognac to each glass and stir.

Add a dash of the sparkling wine and stir gently. Top off with more champagne and serve right away.

Note: Stir the puree and cognac gently; otherwise, the drink can get a little cloudy.

This popcorn is really good! Sweet and salty is a fantastic combination that goes wonderfully well with rosemary. Try it. You won't be disappointed.

Salty-Sweet Rosemary Popcorn

About 6 portions ✦ **10 minutes**

2–3 tablespoons butter
1 tablespoon finely chopped rosemary
1½–2 tablespoons granulated sugar
¾ cup popping corn
Vegetable oil for popping
1–1½ teaspoons salt

Melt the butter together with the rosemary in a small saucepan. Stir in the sugar and put it to the side.

Pop the popcorn in the vegetable oil in a roomy pot with a lid. Stir the herb butter into the warm popcorn, season with salt, and toss everything together thoroughly.

If you have a convection oven, check to see if you have a convection function with bottom heating. This is the secret behind excellent pizza crust without using a baking stone. Mamma mia, what a pizza! Of course, if you have a regular oven this pizza will come out just as well.

Pizza with Chanterelles, Chorizo, and Pecorino

4–6 portions ✦ 30 + 45 minutes

Porcini Salt

⅓ ounce (10 grams) dried porcini mushrooms

SCANT ½ cup flaked sea salt

Pizza Dough

0.4 ounce fresh cake yeast

2 teaspoons honey

1 teaspoon salt

1 cup lukewarm water

2½ tablespoons olive oil

2½ cups all-purpose flour + ¼ cup for baking

Topping

1 yellow onion

2 cloves of garlic

5 ounces chanterelle mushrooms

1½ dried chorizo or another flavorful dried sausage or salami

Butter for frying

Salt and freshly ground black pepper

2 tablespoons roasted red pepper pesto or relish

¾ cup grated pecorino

Blend the dried mushrooms for the porcini salt into a fine powder. Combine the powder and the flaked salt thoroughly and pour it into an airtight jar.

Crumble the yeast for the dough in a bowl. Add the honey, salt, and a little of the water and stir until the yeast has loosened up. Add the rest of the water and olive oil. Stir in the flour, a little at a time, and work together until a smooth dough forms. Knead the dough sufficiently, 5 minutes in an electric mixer with a dough hook, or 10 minutes by hand. Let the dough rise for about 45 minutes under a kitchen towel.

Preheat the oven to 475°F. If you're using a convection oven, use the function with bottom heating. Scatter a little flour on two baking sheets and place them in the oven while it's warming up. Slice the yellow onion and garlic. Cut the large chanterelles into smaller pieces and thinly slice the sausage. Fry the onions, garlic, and chanterelles in butter in a frying pan on medium heat until all the liquid from the mushrooms has cooked off. Season with black pepper.

Tip the dough out onto a floured baking board, divide it into 2–4 portions, and lightly knead them. Roll out the portions into thin crusts and slide them onto floured parchment paper. Spread red pepper pesto over the pizzas and distribute the chanterelle-onion mixture and sausage over the top. Season with salt and pepper and a little porcini salt and sprinkle with pecorino.

Carefully transfer the pizzas from the parchment paper onto the hot baking sheets.

Bake the pizzas in the middle of the oven until the crust is golden brown, about 15 minutes. If using a convection setting, switch it off halfway through the baking time. (This works just as well in a regular oven.) Slice the pizza and serve it right away.

With this salty and creamy miso dip, nutty sesame seeds pair deliciously with crunchy, refreshing cucumbers. First, dip a cucumber spear into the miso dip and then into the sesame seeds. I promise, you won't be able to stop eating this once you start. You can find miso (Japanese soybean paste) in Asian food stores or any well-stocked grocery store, and it keeps for several months, if you store it in a sealed plastic bag in the fridge.

Cucumber with Miso Dip and Roasted Sesame Seeds

4 portions ✦ 5 minutes

4 tablespoons light sesame seeds
2½ tablespoons light (white) miso paste
2½ tablespoons mayonnaise
½ teaspoon sesame oil
2½ tablespoons water
Cucumber spears

Toast the sesame seeds carefully in a dry frying pan, swirling the pan, over low heat. Grind half of the seeds in a mortar or spice grinder. Mix the ground sesame seeds, miso paste, mayonnaise, oil, and water together in a bowl.

Sprinkle several pinches of the toasted whole sesame seeds over the dip. Serve with the cucumber spears and the rest of the sesame seeds.

This pesto-like cilantro and mint dip gives the mild taste of shrimp a real kick. It's very good! The dip can easily be prepared several days in advance.

Shrimp with Cilantro and Mint Dip

4 portions ✦ 10 minutes

½–1 green chile, such as jalapeño or serrano

1 large clove of garlic

1 teaspoon fresh ginger juice

2 teaspoons fish sauce

2 teaspoons freshly squeezed juice from 1 lime (preferably organic)

SCANT ½ cup finely chopped mint

SCANT ½ cup finely chopped cilantro

2 teaspoons granulated sugar

8 ounces cooked, peeled shrimp

Finely chop the chile and garlic, transfer to a bowl, and mix the chile and garlic with the rest of the ingredients, except for the shrimp, until all the sugar has dissolved. Let the dip sit, so that all the flavors can integrate well, for at least 20 minutes before serving.

Serve the dip with the peeled shrimp.

I use smoked pork sausage for these tasty bites. When I'm eating only a small amount of something, I want it to be packed with flavor. These do!

Rye Slices with Creamy Smoked Sausage Spread

8–10 slices ◆ 10 minutes

½ yellow onion
½ pound smoked pork sausage
5 ounces frozen spinach, thawed
 Canola oil for frying
4 ounces cream cheese
1 teaspoon white vinegar
 Salt and black pepper
 Rye bread slices

Thinly slice the onion. Slice the sausage, pull off the casing, and mash the meat coarsely. Squeeze out the majority of the water from the spinach. Heat a frying pan with oil over medium heat and fry the onion, sausage, and spinach together, stirring, for a few minutes.

Let the mixture cool completely and then add it to a food processor with the cream cheese and vinegar and pulse until smooth. Season with salt and pepper.

Use a generous amount of the spread on each slice of rye bread.

If you don't have time to make my Alfajores cookies (page 245), just throw together these little toasts—there's a good story behind them. A while back, after a lot of mingling at a party, I finally ended up at the buffet table, where there wasn't much left, except for a little dulce de leche, some sourdough bread, and a little flaked sea salt. So I simply spread a thick layer of dulce de leche over a slice of sourdough and topped it with the sea salt. I almost fell over, it was so good!

Pane Caramello with Flake Salt

8–10 portions ✦ 5 minutes + 3 hours

1 sourdough baguette, other light sourdough bread, or raisin bread

1 can of dulce de leche (see page 244)
Flaked sea salt

7 ounces (about 1¾ cups) raspberries

Prepare the dulce de leche. Slice and toast the bread. Spread the caramel sauce over each slice of bread and top it with flaked sea salt and raspberries.

End of Summer Picnic

Pumpkin Focaccia with Feta Cheese

Lemon-Stewed Cabbage

Lamb Meatballs

Balsamic-Glazed Red Beets

Mushroom Pesto

Oven-Baked Apples and Onion
with Sweet Chile Bacon

Carrot Dip with Goat Cheese

Pear Cake with Salted Caramel Sauce

When sunset come early and you start reaching for a sweater, you know you're headed for fall. But it's just at this point that the summer pantry is actually at its best—a cornucopia of handpicked mushrooms and root vegetables; fresh, frilly dill; sweet apples; and fat pumpkins. I love it! If there's a time when you should be dining outdoors, this is it, because who knows when it will be the last day of summer? Hurry, hurry!

Don't forget the pumpkins! They are so incredibly good in desserts, salads, and soups—and not least of all, bread. Here, I use sugar pumpkin to top a hearty focaccia. Butternut squash work just as well in this recipe. And when pumpkin season is over? Well, I just toss in carrot instead!

Pumpkin Focaccia with Feta Cheese

About 10 portions ✦ About 2 hours

Topping

1	pound pumpkin meat (about 1½ pounds with the rind)
½	teaspoon salt
⅓	teaspoon red pepper flakes
1½	tablespoons olive oil
1	yellow onion
2	sprigs of rosemary
5	ounces feta cheese made from sheep's or goat's milk
	Flaked sea salt

Dough

0.2	ounce fresh yeast
1½	tablespoons honey
1	teaspoon salt
1½	cups lukewarm water
4	cups all-purpose flour
¼	cup olive oil

Preheat the oven to 425°F using the convection function, if you have it. Cut the pumpkin for the topping into ¾-inch cubes and place them on a baking sheet. Sprinkle salt and red pepper flakes over them, drizzle with olive oil, and toss to combine

thoroughly. Roast the pumpkin in the middle of the oven for 25–30 minutes or until it is soft.

Crumble the yeast for the dough into a bowl. Add the honey, salt, and a little of the water and stir until the yeast has loosened up. Pour in the rest of the water. Stir in the flour, a little at a time, and stir until it forms a smooth dough. Add the oil. Knead the dough sufficiently, 5 minutes in an electric mixer with a dough hook, or 10 minutes by hand. Let rise for about 45 minutes under a kitchen towel.

Switch off the convection setting on the oven, and preheat to 425°F. Grease a large baking sheet, about 11 × 17 inches, with olive oil and line it with parchment paper. Tip the focaccia dough into the pan. Grease your hands with a little olive oil and press the dough out into the edges with your fingers.

Distribute the roasted pumpkin, oil, and red pepper flakes from the other baking sheet onto the top of the dough. Slice the onion and scatter it over the top. Pull off the rosemary leaves and sprinkle them evenly over the pieces of pumpkin. Top with crumbled feta cheese and flaked salt.

Press all of the toppings lightly into the dough. Bake the bread in the middle of the oven until light golden brown, about 35 minutes. Let the bread cool on a rack.

Okay, now that the summer is winding down, it's high time to make use of all the fantastic cabbages that are in their prime! Lemon-stewed cabbage is one of my favorites, and is especially good with sausage or really good, fresh fish.

Lemon-Stewed Cabbage

4 portions ✦ 30 minutes

14 ounces white cabbage
½ stick (4 tablespoons) butter
1 cup whole milk
1 cup heavy cream
3–4 tablespoons cornstarch
Grated zest from 1 lemon (preferably organic)
2 tablespoons freshly squeezed lemon juice
Herb salt
Freshly ground white pepper

Finely shred the cabbage, using even the core if it's tender. If the core is a little tough, you can cook it in some vegetable stock until it softens. Then you only have to slice it and add it to stew when it's ready.

Melt the butter in a large saucepan on medium heat. Add the cabbage and sauté for a few minutes. Add the milk and cream and bring to a boil on low heat while constantly stirring. Let the mixture simmer until the cabbage is soft, and thicken with cornstarch according to the directions on the package.

Flavor the stew with lemon zest and juice, herb salt, and white pepper. Serve with potatoes and parsley and a good sausage.

Poached meatballs are often left in the shadow of their fried cousins. Here I make extraordinarily fine lamb meatballs and flavor them with lemon and oregano before cooking them in white wine and chicken stock.

Lamb Meatballs

4–6 portions ◆ **About 40 minutes**

1 slice of white bread without crusts
4 tablespoons milk
1 yellow onion
2 large cloves of garlic
  Butter for frying
1 pound ground lamb
  Grated zest of 2 lemons (preferably organic)
1 teaspoon fresh lemon juice
SCANT ½ cup chopped oregano, plus additional for topping
  Salt and black pepper

Broth

2 cups chicken stock
1¼ cups dry white wine
8 black peppercorns
5 bay leaves

Dip the bread in milk and crumble it into a large bowl. Finely chop the onion and garlic and sauté in a frying pan with butter on medium heat. Combine the cooled onion mixture with the soaked bread, ground lamb, lemon zest, lemon juice, and oregano. Stir together into a smooth and flexible mixture and season with salt and pepper. Test-fry a small bit to make sure the seasoning is right. Adjust if needed.

In a large saucepan, bring the stock, white wine, pepper, and bay leaves to a boil and let cook for a few minutes. During this time, form the meat mixture into good-sized meatballs. This works best with slightly wet hands.

Place about ⅓ of the meatballs into the simmering stock, and let them cook for about 10 minutes, or until they are completely cooked through. Remove them gently with a slotted spoon and place them in a bowl or pot with the lid on so that they stay warm. Cook the rest of the meatballs in batches.

Strain the liquid, pour it over the meatballs, and serve warm, preferably with a little extra oregano on top.

There is nothing better than cooked red beets coated in warm butter. And with a little balsamic vinegar, they're divine. If possible, use a vinegar with a sweeter, rounder flavor in this recipe.

Balsamic-Glazed Red Beets

4 portions ✦ About 30 minutes

10½ ounces whole red beets
1½ teaspoons salt
⅓ cup brown sugar
SCANT ½ cup balsamic vinegar
3 tablespoons butter
A few leaves of coarsely chopped arugula
(optional)

Peel the beets and cut them roughly into wedges. Place them in a pot and cover with water. Add the salt, brown sugar, and balsamic vinegar and bring to a boil. Boil, covered, until the beets are soft when pierced with a knife. Remove from the heat and let the beets soak in the liquid for 10 minutes. Pour off the liquid.

Melt the butter, pour it over the beets and toss them. Serve the beets warm and, if you like, topped with coarsely chopped arugula.

To make this tasty pesto, use any mix of mushrooms you like. Wild mushrooms or even cremini and portobellos will work beautifully. Chanterelles are another good option. It's fantastic on bread or to toss with pasta or new potatoes. Try it the next time you make a really nice mushroom pizza. Cover the pesto completely with olive oil if you plan to save it in the fridge. It keeps for at least 10 days.

Mushroom Pesto

6–8 portions ✦ About 20 minutes

10½	ounces mixed mushrooms
1	large yellow onion
3	cloves of garlic
2	tablespoons butter
	Salt and black pepper
2	ounces (about ½ cup) pine nuts
4	ounces finely grated, aged cheese, such as Parmesan or pecorino
¾	cup finely chopped parsley
⅓–½	cup olive oil

Rinse and finely chop the mushrooms. Chop the onion and garlic. Heat a frying pan with butter and sauté the garlic, onions, and mushrooms until all the liquid has cooked off. Season with salt and pepper and place everything in a blender or processor together with the pine nuts, cheese, parsley, and a little of the oil.

Mix to a smooth pesto and add the rest of the oil at the end, because the oil has a tendency to become bitter if you over blend it. If you need to, stir in more olive oil to achieve a smooth consistency. Season with salt and pepper and serve.

Food for entertaining is easiest (and tastes best, I would argue) when everything is baked in one dish! This savory casserole looks and tastes fantastic

Oven-Baked Apples
and Onion with Sweet Chile and Bacon

4 portions ✦ About 30 minutes

6 small firm apples

5 small red onions

5 ounces (about 5 strips) bacon

⅔ cup sweet chile sauce

1 tablespoon light soy sauce

Juice of 1 lemon

¼ teaspoon salt

Freshly ground black pepper

1 bunch of parsley, coarsely chopped

Preheat the oven to 425°F. Core and split the apples in half. Split the red onions lengthwise.

Place the bacon strips at the bottom of a small baking dish. Distribute the onions and apples over it. Combine the sweet chile sauce, soy sauce, and lemon juice in a bowl and drizzle the mixture over the apples and onions. Season with salt and ample black pepper.

Bake in the middle of the oven for 25 minutes. Baste the apples and onions with the liquid several times while they're baking. Garnish with parsley and serve warm.

This is a creamy and dangerously good carrot dip that can be served either cold or at room temperature.

Carrot Dip with Goat Cheese

4 portions ◆ About 40 minutes

8	ounces (about 3 medium) carrots
1–2	small cloves of garlic
1½	tablespoons olive oil
	Salt
2	ounces chèvre (fresh goat cheese)
⅔	cup whole milk yogurt
	Grated zest and juice of ⅓ of a lemon (preferably organic)
	Salt and black pepper
	Pita bread for serving
	Fresh cilantro

Preheat the oven to 400°F. Peel the carrots and halve them lengthwise. Place the carrots in a baking dish together with the garlic (still in its skin). Drizzle with the olive oil, salt them, and then roast for about 35 minutes or until the carrots are soft.

Let everything cool some and peel the garlic cloves. In a food processor, puree the carrots, garlic, the oil from the pan, chèvre, and yogurt until smooth. Flavor with lemon juice and zest along with salt and pepper.

Serve the dip at room temperature with warm pita bread and fresh cilantro.

This is one of the best cakes you can bake when pears are in season. Don't be afraid of the flaked sea salt—it absolutely makes this recipe.

Pear Cake with Salted Caramel Sauce

8–10 slices   ✦   About 1 hour and 15 minutes + 30 minutes

2 large pears
5 ounces (about 1 cup) roasted hazelnuts

Cake Batter

1 stick room temperature butter
3 large room temperature eggs
1 cup plus 2 tablespoons granulated sugar
⅓ cup whole milk, at room temperature
2 teaspoons baking powder
1⅔ cups sifted all-purpose flour

Caramel Sauce

¾ cup granulated sugar
¾ cup heavy cream
½ teaspoon flaked sea salt
Flaked sea salt for serving

Preheat the oven to 350°F. Line the sides and bottom of a 9-inch springform pan with parchment paper. This works best if you first brush the pan with a little oil.

Peel, core, and cut the pears into wedges. Combine all the ingredients for the cake batter in a bowl and beat with an electric hand mixer for 5 minutes until smooth. Distribute half of the batter evenly in the springform pan. Place half of the pear wedges along the edges of the pan and cover with the rest of the batter. Finish by placing the rest of the pear wedges along the edge and gently press them down into the batter.

Bake the cake in the lower third of the oven for 55–60 minutes or until the cake has loosened from the edges and begins to feel firm. It's not a problem if the cake is a little moist in the middle when you test with a toothpick. Remove the cake, let it cool briefly, and then loosen and remove the outer ring from the pan.

While the cake is baking, make the caramel sauce. Pour half of the sugar in a large saucepan on low heat and let it melt while stirring. Pour in the remaining sugar and stir until that too has melted. The sugar should just melt and only turn light golden brown. Stir constantly so that it doesn't burn.

Carefully add the cream and stir until the mixture has cooked together into a caramel sauce and any sugar clumps have dissolved. This takes a few minutes.

Remove the pot from the heat and stir in the flaked salt. Coarsely chop the hazelnuts. Pour the caramel sauce over the cake and top with hazelnuts and a little more flaked sea salt.

Note: Before you glaze the cake, put it in the fridge for about 30 minutes, until it is cold. This will make the glaze harden a little and make it easier to get a good-looking cake with beautiful drips down the sides. Pour a little glaze at a time, and work from the middle and out toward the sides with the help of a metal pastry spatula or rubber spatula.

Extra Side Dishes

Early Summer Salad with Cauliflower Crumble

Gnocchi Salad with Pecorino and Pear

Summer's No. 1 Potato Salad
with Browned Butter, Dill, and Chanterelles

Tomato and Strawberry Salad with Basil and Garlic

Bean Salad with Herbs and Halloumi

Nectarine and Snap Pea Salad with Sesame Dressing

Grilled Zucchini with Mozzarella and Pine Nuts

Thai-Style Carrot Salad

Fennel Slaw

South American Rice Salad
with Peaches, Black Beans, and Coriander

Fresh Potato Salad
with Horseradish, Lemon, and Capers

Roasted BBQ Potatoes

Herb and Cheese Baked New Potatoes

Indian Cauliflower Salad with Almonds

Tabbouleh with Parsley and Mint

Pickled Rhubarb

With every season there is a fresh bounty of veggies: Early summer's springy asparagus and crunchy radishes are replaced, eventually, by sweet tomatoes and crispy fennel; and tender zucchini gives way to carrots glowing with color, as the summer nights get shorter. And is there a better time for a variety of delicious cabbages? This is the natural rhythm. The beautiful thing is that there is always something really good to eat from the vegetable garden. Here are some of my favorite side dishes, because you can never have enough good ideas for the abundance of fresh summer vegetables.

I'm a sucker for contrasts: Warm and cold, sweet and salty, and, last but not least, smooth and crunchy. This has led me to wonder if warm, crumbled cauliflower florets might be the perfect contrast to the cool veggies in this summer salad. I believe they are!

Early Summer Salad with Cauliflower Crumble

4 portions ✦ About 10 minutes

1 bundle of green asparagus
½ cucumber
1 red onion
3½ ounces (about 1½ cups) sugar snap peas
ABOUT 2 ounces (about 1½ cups) mixed salad greens
⅓ head of cauliflower (about 7 ounces)
Grated zest of 1 lemon (preferably organic)
Flaked sea salt and black pepper

Dressing
SCANT ½ cup Greek whole milk yogurt
SCANT ½ cup finely grated parmesan cheese
Grated zest of ½ lemon (preferably organic)
1 tablespoon freshly squeezed lemon juice
1 tablespoon Dijon mustard
Salt and black pepper
Water

Bring a large pot of salted water to a boil. Break off the tough ends of the asparagus, if they are hard, and boil the remaining stalks until al dente, about 2 minutes. Drain, peel, seed, and slice the cucumber into thick pieces. Finely slice the onion. Slice the sugar snap peas into thick strips. Add the salad greens and toss everything together in a bowl.

To make the dressing, whisk together all the dressing ingredients, except for the water. Whisk in the water until you have reached the desired consistency, and season with salt and black pepper.

Coarsely chop the cauliflower until crumbly, either in a food processor or with a sharp knife. Roast the cauliflower crumbles briefly in a dry frying pan on high heat until they get a little color. Remove from heat and stir in the lemon zest.

Toss the salad and top with the cauliflower crumble. Serve with the dressing, flaked salt, and black pepper on the side. I prefer the crumble to be room temperature, but the salad is just as good served cold.

In Tuscany, I once had a simple, but fantastically good salad that consisted only of flavorful pecorino, soft pears, olive oil, and ample black pepper. Here, I have expanded the salad by adding store-bought potato gnocchi. This dish is excellent with meat, poultry, fish (especially oily varieties), and sausage.

Gnocchi Salad
with Pecorino and Pear

4 portions ✦ **About 15 minutes**

2 small cloves of garlic
1½ tablespoons good olive oil
2 tablespoons chopped, fresh rosemary
1 bag of fresh gnocchi (about 1 pound)
2 soft ripe pears, such as Anjou or Bosc, peeled
   Flake salt and coarsely ground black pepper
   Good amount of grated pecorino

Finely chop the garlic. Heat a frying pan with olive oil and sauté the garlic on low heat. Remove the pan from heat, fold in the rosemary and let cool.

Boil the gnocchi in salted water for a few minutes until they have floated up to the surface. While the gnocchi are cooking, core the pears and coarsely cube them. Pour off the water and blend the gnocchi gently in the pot with the garlic and rosemary oil along with the pears. Season with salt and pepper and pour into a serving bowl.

Top with pecorino and serve immediately, preferably with a little extra cheese on the side, so people can add more if they like.

Here you have the summer's surest bet—a potato salad so good that I eat it like candy. The secret? The butter, of course. If you don't have chanterelles on hand, you can leave them out.

Summer's No. 1 Potato Salad with Browned Butter, Dill, and Chanterelles

4 portions ✦ **About 20 minutes**

1⅓   pounds waxy potatoes

7   tablespoons butter

6   ounces chanterelle mushrooms, chopped
Flaked sea salt

⅔   cup chopped dill

Wash the potatoes, boil them until soft in salted water, and pour them into a bowl. Melt 5 tablespoons of the butter in a pot on medium heat and let it simmer until it is golden brown and begins to smell a little nutty. Remove the pot from the heat and let the melted butter sit for a few minutes. While the butter in the pot is cooling, sauté the chanterelles in the remaining butter over medium heat until golden and season with salt.

Pour the melted butter through a fine-mesh sieve to strain out the brown residue. Fold the dill into the butter and combine with the freshly cooked potatoes. Top with the chanterelles and season with flaked salt. Serve immediately.

This is exactly my type of summer food: simple, quick, and full of flavor. And it's also good with just about everything on the grill.

Tomato and Strawberry Salad with Basil and Garlic

4 portions ✦ 10 minutes

8 ounces strawberries

10½ ounces (about 2 cups) small cherry tomatoes

About 15 basil leaves

1 clove of garlic

1 tablespoon olive oil

Flaked sea salt and coarsely ground black pepper

Halve the strawberries and tomatoes. Slice the basil leaves into small pieces and finely chop the garlic. Toss everything together with the olive oil in a serving bowl. Season with salt and black pepper.

I use thin green beans and wax beans in this recipe, but use whatever beans are in season. If you're grilling in winter, this salad works just as well with frozen beans, and you can find Halloumi cheese in just about any supermarket these days.

Bean Salad
with Herbs and Halloumi

4 portions ✦ 10 minutes

5 ounces thin green beans
5 ounces yellow wax beans
⅓ cup olive oil, plus more for cooking
⅔ cup chopped fresh herbs (e.g., oregano, thyme, and basil)
1 small clove of garlic, grated
7 ounces Halloumi cheese
   Flaked sea salt and coarsely ground black pepper

Bring a saucepan of salted water to a boil. Trim the beans and cook them quickly in the boiling water until they are soft but still crisp. Drain and place the beans in a large bowl. Stir together the oil, herbs, and garlic and blend the dressing with the warm beans.

Slice the Halloumi into thin slices. Heat a frying pan with olive oil over medium heat and fry the Halloumi for about 1 minute on each side or until it is light golden brown. Combine the Halloumi with the beans, season with salt and black pepper, and serve.

On a trip to Japan, I fell in love with sesame: sesame oil, roasted sesame seeds, ground sesame seeds . . . they're incredibly good in just about every way. A little heat, sweetness, and nuttiness makes this salad, tossed with sesame dressing, the perfect side dish for lighter grilled fare such as fish, shellfish, and chicken. But try it with grilled pork loin or ribs, too.

Nectarine and Snap Pea Salad with Sesame Dressing

4 portions ✦ 15 minutes

3	tablespoons sesame seeds
4	ripe nectarines
3½	ounces snap peas
½	red onion
1	tablespoon canola oil
1	teaspoon sesame oil
	Juice from ½ lemon
½	teaspoon honey
	Coarsely ground black pepper
1	cup fresh baby spinach leaves
	Flake salt

Toast the sesame seeds in a dry pan on medium heat until they have a nice light brown color. They burn easily, so keep an eye on the pan.

Split the nectarines lengthwise, remove the pits, and cut into wedges. Thinly slice the snap peas lengthwise. Thinly slice the onion.

Finely grind half of the roasted sesame seeds, either in a spice grinder or a food processor, and stir them together with the canola oil, sesame oil, lemon juice, and honey. Season the dressing with ample black pepper.

Toss the nectarines, snap peas, red onion, and spinach in the dressing in a serving bowl. Season with flaked salt and top with the rest of the sesame seeds.

Whenever I grill slices of zucchini, I want them to be tender on the inside and smoky and charred on the outside. To achieve this, the coals should be at a medium heat. If they're too hot, the zucchini will burn quickly, and if it's not hot enough, you won't get a char-grilled skin. Here, I finish the dish with mozzarella, but feta cheese is just as good.

Grilled Zucchini with Mozzarella and Pine Nuts

4 portions ◆ About 15 minutes

¼–⅓ cup pine nuts
1 pound zucchini
2 tablespoons olive oil
Flaked sea salt and coarsely ground black pepper
2–3 sprigs fresh oregano
4 ounces fresh mozzarella

Toast the pine nuts in a dry pan over medium heat until they are golden brown. They burn easily, so keep your eye on the pan.

Cut the zucchini into ¼-inch-thick slices. Brush them with olive oil on both sides and season with salt and pepper. Grill the zucchini slices for about 2 minutes on each side or until they are charred but still firm. While the zucchini is cooking, pull the oregano leaves from the sprigs.

Arrange the zucchini on a serving platter. Top with pine nuts and oregano leaves. Tear the mozzarella into pieces and distribute it evenly over the top.

This fresh, crispy salad is usually made with green papaya—a traditional dish in both Laos and Thailand—but it works just as well with carrots or radishes. The trick to making this salad especially good is in the grinding. The finer the grind, the greater the flavor. Use a box grater or mandoline for the veggies.

Thai-Style Carrot Salad

4 portions ✦ 15 minutes

1   pound carrots or green papaya
½   red chile, such as Fresno, stemmed
     and seeded
2   cloves of garlic
½   teaspoon salt
1½   tablespoons granulated sugar
     Juice from 1 lime
3   tablespoons fish sauce

Peel the carrots and coarsely grate them on a box grater or thinly slice them with a mandoline and cut them into matchsticks. Put them in a large bowl.

Coarsely chop the chile and garlic and mash in a mortar together with the salt and sugar. Grind together thoroughly and add the lime juice and fish sauce. Continue to grind until a smooth paste is formed.

Add the paste to the carrots and toss for a moment or two so that everything blends together. Season and add more lime juice or fish sauce, if desired.

Fennel is at its best in the middle of the summer, when I eat it sliced and tossed with lemon juice, olive oil, and flaked sea salt, almost every day. You can also use this recipe to make a creamy slaw with just a hint of orange. You can save the tougher parts of the fennel bulb for recipes that give them time to soften—in pasta sauce, soup, or fish stew.

Fennel Slaw

4 portions ◆ 10 minutes

1 large fennel bulb
   Heaping ¾ cup Greek yogurt
1 tablespoon Dijon mustard
   Grated zest from ½ orange
1 teaspoon white wine vinegar
1 tablespoon mayonnaise
1 teaspoon granulated sugar
   Salt and coarsely ground black pepper

Halve the fennel lengthwise, rinse, and cut away the hard core in the middle. Thinly slice the fennel and combine with the rest of the ingredients in a bowl. Season with salt and pepper.

Fresh and filling at the same time, this salad is excellent with grilled chicken or fish.

South American Rice Salad
with **Peaches**, **Black Beans**, and **Coriander**

4 portions ◆ About 25 minutes

1¼ cups Arborio rice
½ red chile, such as Fresno, stemmed
  and seeded
2 tablespoons canola oil
2 cloves of garlic
  Juice and zest from 2 limes
3 ripe peaches
2 scallions
1 can of black beans (about 14 ounces)
½ cup coarsely chopped cilantro
  Flaked sea salt and coarsely ground
  black pepper

Boil the rice until soft. Drain through a fine-mesh strainer and pour into a large bowl. Finely chop the chile and whisk it in a small bowl together with the olive oil. Grate the garlic into the mixture. Add the lime zest and juice and whisk well. Pour the dressing over the rice and stir gently. Put it to the side and let cool.

Halve and pit the peaches and cut them into wedges. Thinly slice the scallions. Rinse the beans thoroughly in a strainer and fold them into the rice salad together with the peach wedges, scallions, and cilantro. Season with salt and pepper.

Serve the salad cold or at room temperature, preferably with some fresh cilantro leaves on top.

If I'm inviting the whole gang over for a grilled dinner, this creamy potato salad perfectly fits the bill. It doesn't contain any mayonnaise, so it's not as heavy as the traditional salad—after all, you want to have some room for other dishes. And if you're like me, a friend of horseradish, feel free to top the potato salad with a liberal handful of freshly grated horseradish when it's time to serve.

Fresh Potato Salad
with Horseradish, Lemon, and Capers

4 portions ✦ About 25 minutes

1⅓ pounds waxy potatoes
⅔ cup sour cream
1 tablespoon Dijon mustard
½ teaspoon honey
2 tablespoons finely grated fresh horseradish
Grated zest from 1 lemon
Flaked sea salt and coarsely ground black pepper
1 small red onion
¾ cup large brined capers, drained
Additional finely grated fresh horseradish, for serving (optional)

Wash the potatoes and boil them until soft in salted water. Drain the potatoes and let them sit until they are cool enough to handle. Cut the potatoes into bite-sized pieces.

In another bowl, stir together the sour cream, mustard, honey, horseradish, and lemon zest. Season with salt and pepper. Stir the dressing into the warm potatoes and combine thoroughly. Finely chop the red onion and scatter it, along with the capers, over the potatoes. Top with more grated horseradish, if you like.

You can make these delicious BBQ potatoes as hot as you like by adjusting the amount of adobo sauce. Cut the potatoes into wedges, if they are large, but if they're small, just roast them as they are.

Roasted BBQ Potatoes

4 portions ✦ About 40 minutes

2 red peppers
1⅓ pounds waxy potatoes
2 cloves of garlic
½ teaspoon adobo sauce from canned chipotles
½–1 teaspoon mild paprika powder (or smoked paprika powder)
2 tablespoons canola oil
Flake salt and coarsely ground black pepper

Preheat the oven to 425°F.

Stem, seed, and cut the peppers into rough wedges. Wash the potatoes and, if you want, cut them into wedges. Finely chop the garlic and place it together with the potatoes and peppers in an oven-safe pan. Stir together the adobo sauce, paprika powder, and oil in a small bowl, then pour it over the potatoes and peppers and toss to coat. Season with salt and pepper.

Roast the mixture in the middle of the oven for about 30 minutes or until the potatoes feel soft and everything begins to brown. You can also turn the broiler on at the end of the cooking time to help the potatoes crisp. Serve immediately.

We all know that the absolute best thing you can do with a potato is to eat it freshly boiled with a generous dollop of salted butter on top. But baked potatoes are especially good with cheese. And herbs. And . . . Oh, why not throw it all in at the same time!

Herb and Cheese Baked New Potatoes

4 portions ◆ 45 minutes

1¾	pounds new potatoes or small red potatoes, cut in half
½	teaspoon salt
1¾	ounces (about ½ cup) grated aged Swiss, cheddar, or Gouda cheese
2	tablespoons room temperature butter
SCANT ½	cup chopped fresh oregano
½	teaspoon salt
	Black pepper

Preheat the oven to 425°F. Place the potatoes, skin side down, in a small baking dish. Sprinkle salt over them and roast the potatoes in the middle of the oven for 30–35 minutes or until they are almost totally soft.

Meantime, stir together the cheese, butter, oregano, salt, and pepper for the topping. Remove the baking dish from the oven and top each potato with the mixture.

Preheat the broiler and broil the potatoes for about 10 minutes or until the potatoes are soft and the topping has browned.

Using different kinds of nuts can transform this salad. Try it with grilled chicken,
good sausage, or lamb with some Indian flavors. You won't be disappointed.

Indian Cauliflower Salad with Almonds

4 portions ✦ 10 minutes

½ cup whole blanched almonds (about
  3 ounces)
14 ounces cauliflower
 1 teaspoon garam masala
 1 teaspoon cumin
½–1 teaspoon chile flakes
 1 tablespoon canola oil
 3 tablespoons freshly pressed apple juice
½ teaspoon honey
  Salt and coarsely ground black pepper

Toast the almonds, tossing frequently in a dry pan
over medium heat until they are light golden brown.
They burn easily, so keep your eye on the pan.

Bring a large saucepan of salted water to a boil.
Split the cauliflower into small florets. Boil the
cauliflower until it is crisp-tender, 4–5 minutes.
Drain thoroughly in a colander.

Meantime, whisk together the spices, oil, apple
juice, and honey into a dressing. Toss the cooked
cauliflower florets with the dressing in a serving
bowl and season with salt and pepper.

Coarsely chop the almonds and sprinkle them
over the salad. Serve the salad warm or cold.

Whenever I eat Lebanese mezze, there is a dish I can't get enough of—tabbouleh. Usually it's made with bulgur wheat, but here I use wheat berries. I also like a lot of parsley, mint, and lemon juice in my tabbouleh, and I serve it with grilled sausages as well as lamb, beef, and pork. This filling salad is even better the second day, so make a generous batch of it.

Tabbouleh with Parsley and Mint

4 portions ◆ 15 + 30 minutes

2 cloves of garlic

1 red onion

½ cucumber

3 large tomatoes, seeds removed

1⅔ cups cooked wheat berries (cooked in vegetable stock)

Juice and grated zest from 1 lemon

¼ cup good olive oil

SCANT ½ cup chopped mint

⅔ cup chopped parsley

Salt and coarsely ground black pepper

Finely chop the garlic, red onion, cucumber, and tomato. Combine everything with the wheat berries, lemon juice and zest, and olive oil in a serving bowl. Fold the herbs into the mixture and season with salt and pepper.

Let the tabbouleh sit for at least 30 minutes before serving.

There is nothing I long for as much as the season's first rhubarb. In pies, cakes, soups, sauces, marmalade, lemonade . . . there is no end to all the possibilities. Here is a rhubarb recipe so good and beautiful that you must promise to try it. It is lightning-fast to make and tastes fabulously good with just about everything—especially scrambled eggs and smoked fish.

Pickled Rhubarb

6 portions ✦ **About 15 minutes**

3½	ounces rhubarb
¼	cup white vinegar
SCANT ½	cup granulated sugar
⅔	cup water

Slice the rhubarb into thin ribbons lengthwise with a potato peeler or mandoline. In a nonreactive saucepan, bring the vinegar, sugar, and water to a boil, and let it simmer until the sugar has dissolved. Add the rhubarb ribbons, cover, and remove from the heat. Let the liquid cool.

Pour everything into a clean jar and keep it in the fridge, where the rhubarb will last for about 10 days.

Extra Desserts

Panna Cotta Pie with Summer Berries

Cold-Risen Rhubarb with Vanilla Buns

Italian Almond Cookies

Cardamom Crisps

Chocolate Pie with
Muscovado Caramel and Currant

Chocolate Divine with
Grappa-Marinated Strawberries

Dulce de Leche

Alfajores with Dulce de Leche

Grilled Peaches with Honey Yogurt
and Nuts

Pound Cake Bruschetta with
Elderflower and Rhubarb Compote

Chocolatey Jitterbugs

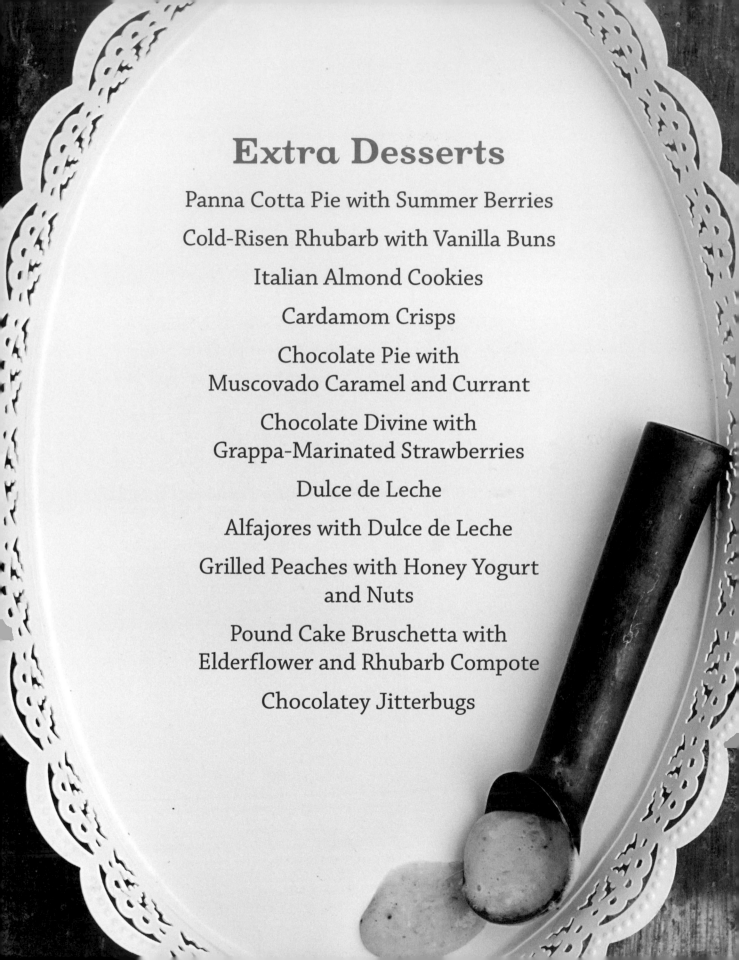

I have a real sweet tooth and want to finish every meal with dessert, whether it's a fancy chocolate cake or a quickly made fruit salad. During the warm summer months, I prefer to make quick desserts tossed together with whatever I happen to have at home, like grilled fruit or pound cake, a cooling sorbet, some crispy cookies, or a rich chocolate sauce.

There's a reason why the creamy Italian dream called panna cotta is the favorite at a large party: it's easy to make and flavor any way you like. In this recipe, I use only fine vanilla beans and use the panna cotta *as pie filling. Just before serving, I scatter an assortment of fresh summer berries over the top. It's so simple and yet so insanely good!*

Panna Cotta Pie with Summer Berries

About 8–10 portions　◆　**40 + 35 minutes**

Pie Dough

SCANT 2　cups all-purpose flour
　　¼　cup confectioners' sugar
　　½　teaspoon salt
　　1　stick cold butter
　　1　small egg

Egg Wash

　　1　whipped egg white
　　1　teaspoon heavy cream or milk

Filling

　4½　gelatin sheets (about 1 rounded table-spoon powdered gelatin, such as Knox)
　1–2　vanilla beans
　3¼　cups whipping cream
　　⅔　cup granulated sugar
　　1　pint berries in season

Combine all the dry ingredients for the pie dough in a bowl or food processor. Cut the butter into cubes and work them into the dry ingredients to form a crumbly mixture. Add the egg and work it in quickly to form a dough.

Roll out the dough into a circle (slightly less than ⅛-inch thick) on a sheet of parchment paper with a little flour, then roll up the paper into a roll and let it chill in the fridge for 20 minutes.

Cover a 9-inch springform pan with the pie dough. Prick the bottom and let the pie dough rest in the fridge for 20 minutes. Meanwhile, heat the oven to 425°F.

Bake the pie shell in the middle of the oven for 12–15 minutes or until it begins to get some color. Mix the egg white and cream for the egg wash and immediately brush the warm bottom of the pie crust with the mixture. This seals the tiny holes in the bottom of the crust so that the filling doesn't leak out. Let the pie shell cool.

Place the gelatin sheets for the filling in cold water and let them soak for 10 minutes. Split the vanilla beans lengthwise and scrape out the seeds. Place the seeds and the scraped beans in a pot together with the cream and sugar and bring to a boil. Remove the pot from the heat and transfer the gelatin sheets to the pot. Stir the mixture with a spoon and let it rest for about 20 minutes, stirring occasionally.

Remove the vanilla beans with a slotted spoon and pour the mixture into the pie crust. Cover the pie with plastic wrap and let it chill in the fridge at least three hours or until the filling has solidified. Top the pie with berries just before you serve it.

I learned just about everything I know about baking from my grandmother. In this recipe, I use her method of "cold rising"—and plenty of butter, which has always been her recommendation when it comes to making buns.

Cold-Risen Rhubarb and Vanilla Buns

30 buns   ✦   30 minutes + 1¼ hours

Filling

1	vanilla bean
7	ounces rhubarb (about 2 stalks)
½	cup granulated sugar
3½	ounces grated almond paste
2	tablespoons room temperature butter
	Water
	Granulated sugar

Dough

1½	sticks butter
4–4¼	cups all-purpose flour
1¾	ounces fresh yeast
1	cup cold whole milk
1	large egg
¼	cup light corn syrup
½	teaspoon salt

To make the filling, split the vanilla bean lengthwise, scrape out the seeds, and place the seeds and the bean in a non-reactive saucepan. Thinly slice the rhubarb and place it in the pot. Bring the mixture to a boil and add the sugar when the rhubarb begins to release its juices. Lower the heat and continue to simmer the rhubarb uncovered for about 15 minutes.

Remove the rhubarb mixture from the heat and let it cool down. Take out the vanilla bean and stir in the almond paste along with the butter. Blend the mixture carefully and set it aside.

To make the dough, work the butter into the flour, either in a food processor or on a work surface, using a knife or fork, until you get pea-sized clumps of dough.

Crumble the yeast in a bowl and stir it together with the milk. Add the egg, corn syrup, and salt to the bowl and stir it all together.

Gradually work the flour mixture into the liquid until it is smooth, using a food processor for about 5 minutes, or by hand in a bowl for about 10 minutes.

Transfer the dough onto a floured work surface and divide into two portions. Knead one portion for a few minutes and then thinly roll it into the shape of a rectangle, 12 × 20 inches, and about ⅛-inch thick. Cut the rectangle into 4 × 4 inch squares and place a heaping tablespoon of filling in the middle of every square. Fold the dough edges over the filling and carefully pinch them together so that the filling won't run out. Turn the filled bun over, seam side down, and form into a round ball. Repeat with the remaining dough and filling. Arrange the buns so they are nearly touching on a parchment-lined baking sheet.

Let the buns rise at room temperature under a clean dishtowel until they double in size, after about 1½ hours. Then preheat the oven to 425°F.

Bake the buns in the middle of the oven for about 8 minutes and let them cool on a rack under the towel. Brush the buns with a little water and dip them in granulated sugar while they are still a little warm.

Despite my German-sounding last name, my heart, which ought to belong to the land of sauerkraut and wurst, belongs to Italy—especially to these fabulous Italian almond cookies. Ti amo amarettini!

Italian Almond Cookies

About 25 cookies ✦ **30 minutes**

  7 ounces (about 1½ cups) whole almonds
  ½ cup granulated sugar
  1 drop almond extract
1½ tablespoons amaretto or almond liqueur
  2 large egg whites
     Confectioners' sugar
  2 tablespoons all-purpose flour, if needed
     (optional)

Preheat the oven to 400°F. Grind the almonds in a food processor for a few minutes until finely chopped. Do not over-grind or the almonds will turn to paste. In a bowl, combine the almonds, sugar, and almond extract. Stir in the amaretto or almond liqueur and one egg white at a time. The batter can get very sticky, depending on the size of the eggs you're using. Add a little flour, if you like, to make the batter a bit more cohesive and less sticky.

Pour the confectioners' sugar onto a deep plate. Form about 1 tablespoon of the relatively sticky batter into a rough ball and roll it in the confectioners' sugar. Repeat with the rest of the batter and place the balls, with space in between them, on a baking sheet lined with parchment paper.

Bake the dough in the middle of the oven for 14–16 minutes. The cookies should be light golden brown but a little chewy in the middle.

Note: No almond liqueur? Use freshly pressed apple juice instead.

I made these crisps for the first time by mistake! They were supposed to be more like biscotti. But the telephone rang, and I forgot they were in the oven. Luckily, they turned out quite wonderfully!

Cardamom Crisps

50–60 crisps ✦ 15 + 25 minutes

1⅔ cups all-purpose flour
⅔ cup granulated sugar
2 teaspoons freshly ground cardamom pods
2 teaspoons baking powder
½ teaspoon salt
7 tablespoons room temperature butter
⅓ cup heavy cream
   Equal parts granulated sugar and freshly ground cardamom in which to roll the cookies
7 ounces dark chocolate

Preheat the oven to 350°F.

Combine all the dry ingredients in a food processor fitted with the stainless steel blade. Cut the butter into cubes, add them to the food processor, and pulse together until crumbly. Add the cream and pulse until the dough starts to come together. Turn the dough out onto a work surface and quickly knead it together. It also works well to make this dough by hand in a bowl.

Form the dough into balls, about ¾-inch in diameter, and roll them in the sugar and cardamom mixture. Place the balls, with a little space between them, on a baking sheet lined with parchment paper and bake in the middle of the oven for about 25 minutes.

Let the cookie crisps cool. Chop the chocolate and melt it over a water bath. Then dip half of each cookie in the melted chocolate.

Lock the door, throw away the key, and dig into these heavenly chocolate pies. Or, if you're feeling generous, make a huge batch of them and invite some friends for coffee.

Chocolate Pie with Muscovado Caramel and Currant

8–9 small pies or 1 large one ✦ **1 hour + 35 minutes**

Pie Dough

1⅔	cups all-purpose flour, plus additional for rolling
3	tablespoons cocoa powder
2	tablespoons confectioners' sugar
½	teaspoon salt
1	stick cold butter
1	small egg

Filling

5	tablespoons butter
1	cup heavy cream
1½	cups dark Muscovado sugar
⅓	cup light corn syrup
	About 1 teaspoon flaked sea salt

For Serving

Red or white currants
Whipped cream
Greek yogurt

Combine all the dry ingredients for the pie dough in a food processor. Cut the butter into cubes, add it to the food processor, and pulse until small clumps form. Add the egg and pulse the food processor until the dough begins to come together. You can also do this by hand in a bowl.

Knead the dough until it is smooth and roll it out thinly (about ⅛-inch) into a round on a piece of parchment paper sprinkled with a little flour. Roll the paper into a cylinder and chill the dough in the fridge for 20 minutes.

Cover either mini pie pans or a 9-inch springform pan with the pie dough. Prick the bottom and let rest in the fridge for 25 minutes.

Preheat the oven to 425°F. Bake the pie shells in the middle of the oven for 15–20 minutes. Let the shells cool and then carefully remove them from the pans.

Combine all the ingredients except the flaked salt for the caramel filling in a heavy-bottomed saucepan. Bring to a boil and then simmer uncovered for 20–30 minutes, either until the batter passes the ball test (drop a little caramel batter in a glass of cold water; if you can form the soft caramel into a little ball with your fingers, it's ready) or until the temperature is 244°F. The time will vary depending on the type of pan you're using. Keep in mind that the caramel should be really soft, so stir it often and don't cook it too long. Stir in the flaked salt, pour the caramel filling into the pie shells, and let it solidify.

Serve the pies with currants and whipped cream blended with yogurt.

Note: Did the pie shell crack during baking? If so, whip together one tablespoon of cream and egg white and brush the pie shell with it. Then put it in a warm oven a few minutes. This will seal any holes.

This is a luxurious cake, full of decadent goodness and perfect for special occasions—or any occasion, really, when your body is screaming for chocolate!

Chocolate Divine
with Grappa-Marinated Strawberries

10–12 slices ✦ **40 + 30 minutes**

14 ounces high-quality dark chocolate

1½ sticks (12 tablespoons) room temperature butter

SCANT ½ cup cane sugar

5 large egg yolks

½ cup all-purpose flour

½ teaspoon salt

¼ cup whole milk

5 large egg whites

Grappa-Marinated Strawberries

9 ounces fresh strawberries

¼ cup water

¼ cup granulated sugar

2 tablespoons grappa

For Serving

Ice cream or whipped cream

Preheat the oven to 350°F. Line the bottom and sides of a 9-inch springform pan with parchment paper. This works best if you brush the pan with a little water or oil first.

Chop and melt the chocolate over a water bath. Whip the butter and sugar until creamy with a hand mixer in a bowl. Whisk in the egg yolks, one at a time. Sift in the flour and add the salt. Pour in the milk and melted chocolate and whip it all together until smooth.

In a clean bowl, whip the egg whites into firm peaks with an electric mixer. Fold the egg whites into the batter with the help of a spatula. Fold gently until everything is completely blended. With a spatula, spread the chocolate batter evenly in the prepared pan and press down a little extra in the middle. This will prevent the center of the cake from sinking when it's baked.

Bake the cake in the middle of the oven for 30–35 minutes. At this point, the cake will feel firm around the rim, but a little looser in the middle. Shortening the baking time gives the cake a wonderfully muddy texture; increasing the time gives you a more solid cake. Remove the cake and let it cool in the pan.

Cut the strawberries in quarters. Bring the water and sugar to a boil in a saucepan and cook until the sugar dissolves. Remove from the heat and add the grappa. Cool to room temperature. Add the strawberries, and let them soak in the marinade for about 20 minutes. Distribute them over the cake and serve with ice cream or whipped cream.

Note: The cake is best if it is baked a day in advance, but marinate the strawberries just before serving.

The caramel cream, dulce de leche, is perfect as an ice cream topping, a cookie filling, or a topping for pancakes, with berries and fruit. A well-stocked supermarket or specialty food store will carry ready-made dulce de leche, but it's easy to make it yourself with sweetened condensed milk. When you are making dulce de leche, it is critical to keep the unopened can of sweetened condensed milk completely covered with water the entire time it is simmering, not boiling!

Dulce de Leche

About ¾ cup ✦ 2–3 hours

1   can of sweetened condensed milk
     (14 ounces)

Set the can of unsweetened condensed milk in a large pot and completely cover the can with water. Bring the water to a boil, lower the heat, and let it simmer for 2–3 hours, covered. It is really important to keep the water simmering, not boiling. Fill the pot with warm water as needed while it's cooking.

Simmering the can for 2–2½ hours is enough, if you want a caramel sauce for ice cream, flan, banana cake, or pie. Cooking it longer, for about 3 hours, works well and yields great fillings for alfajores and other cookies.

Remove the hot can, rinse it in cold water, and let it cool. Open the can with a can opener. Enjoy!

During a trip to Argentina, I was served these cookies more or less around the clock, and I still couldn't get enough. The cookies are less sweet than the dulce de leche *filling, so if you want to eat the cookies without the filling, I suggest that you increase the amount of sugar.*

Alfajores with Dulce de Leche

18 double-sided cookies ✦ About 40 minutes

Cookies

- 7 tablespoons butter at room temperature
- ¼ cup granulated sugar
- 1 tablespoon whole milk
- ½ teaspoon freshly squeezed lemon juice
- 1 cup finely ground cornmeal (fine polenta)
- ¼ cup all-purpose flour
- 1 teaspoon vanilla sugar
- ½ teaspoon baking powder

Filling

- 1 can dulce de leche (see page 244)
- ¾ cup flaked dried coconut (desiccated)

Preheat the oven to 350°F.

In the bowl of an electric mixer fitted with a dough hook, mix the butter and sugar together on medium speed until creamy. Add the milk and lemon juice. In a separate bowl combine the cornmeal, flour, vanilla sugar, and baking powder and stir it into the batter. Mix the ingredients briefly until a dough forms. Wrap the dough tightly in plastic wrap and let it chill in the refrigerator for 25 minutes.

Divide the dough into 36 pieces and roll them into balls. Place the balls, with plenty of room between them, on a baking sheet lined with parchment paper, and flatten them lightly with your hand.

Bake the cookies in the middle of the oven for 15–17 minutes, or until they begin to brown on the edges. Let the cookies cool completely.

Spread a generous amount of *dulce de leche* over half of the cookies and put the other halves on top of them. Roll the sides of each cookie in coconut so that it covers the filling.

When peaches are their best—sweet, juicy and sun-ripened—I prefer to eat them whole, just as they are. At other times, when the harvest isn't quite as perfect, you might need to fiddle a little to bring out their juicy sweetness. In this recipe for grilled peaches, the combination of orange honey and glowing charcoal creates a little magic of its own.

When the coals are still glowing nicely, and everyone starts craving something sweet, this is a perfect light dessert that can be pulled from the fridge and quickly grilled, after the main dishes have been enjoyed.

Grilled Peaches with Honey Yogurt and Nuts

4 portions   ✦   10 + 30 minutes

4 large ripe peaches (or nectarines)
  Juice and zest from ½ orange
¼ cup honey
½ cup Greek yogurt
3½ ounces (about ¾ cup) toasted nuts, such as almonds or pistachios
  Confectioners' sugar for dusting

Halve the peaches through the stem and remove the pit. Gently heat the orange juice, orange zest, and half of the honey in a small saucepan. Remove from the heat, add in the peach halves and marinate them in the orange honey for 30 minutes. It doesn't matter if you marinate them longer. After 15 minutes, turn over the peaches so that they will marinate evenly.

While the peaches are marinating, stir the remaining honey into the yogurt. Coarsely chop the nuts.

Grill the peaches for a few minutes on each side, over low heat, until they are lightly charred all over. Move the peaches to a serving dish and pour over the rest of the marinade. Top the peaches with the honey yogurt and nuts, and dust with confectioners' sugar. Serve and enjoy!

Homemade pound cake flavored with cardamom is wonderfully good, and the flavor goes particularly well with rhubarb compote and ricotta. You can find elderflower syrup, the magic ingredient in this recipe, online or in specialty food stores.

Pound Cake Bruschetta with Elderflower and Rhubarb Compote

4 portions ✦ 20 minutes

1 pound rhubarb
¾ cup concentrated elderflower syrup
SCANT ½ cup granulated sugar
7 ounces ricotta
¼ cup confectioners' sugar
1 teaspoon vanilla sugar
4 slices day-old pound cake (your own or store bought)

Thinly slice the rhubarb and bring it to a boil in a saucepan along with the elderflower syrup and granulated sugar. Let the mixture simmer, covered, over medium heat for 10–15 minutes, and then pour the hot compote into a clean, heated glass jar.

Stir together the ricotta, confectioners' sugar, and vanilla sugar.

Grill the pound cake slices briefly on both sides over low heat. Watch the cake carefully so that it doesn't burn. Spread the ricotta over the warm cake slices and top them off with the rhubarb compote. Delicious.

Making jitterbugs is a sticky business that results in an unbelievably good shortbread cookie. My grandma Lilly's jitterbugs are my absolute favorite. The secret to making these cookies so good is doubling the meringue. I've also tossed in a little melted chocolate. Could any sweet treat be any better than this?

Chocolaty Jitterbugs

30–34 cookies ✦ 20 minutes + 1½ hours

Shortbread

- 1¾ sticks (14 tablespoons) cold butter
- ¼ cup granulated sugar
- SCANT 2 cups all-purpose flour
- ¼ teaspoon of salt
- 1 large egg yolk

Meringue

- 3½ ounces high-quality dark chocolate
- ½ teaspoon of salt
- 3 large egg whites
- ⅔ cup granulated sugar
- ⅛ teaspoon white vinegar

For the shortbread cookies, cut the butter into cubes and work it quickly together with the remaining ingredients until small clumps form. Feel free to use a food processor. Split the dough into two portions. Knead them lightly, and then flatten them. Wrap the dough tightly in plastic and let it rest in the fridge for about 25 minutes.

For the meringue, chop the chocolate and melt it over a water bath. Stir the salt into the chocolate, remove it from the heat, and let it cool to room temperature. Beat the egg whites and ⅓ of the sugar to stiff peaks with a hand mixer on low speed. Add the rest of the sugar and vinegar and continue to beat under increased speed until it becomes a shiny and firm meringue. Gently fold the chocolate into the meringue.

On a piece of parchment, roll out one portion of shortbread into an 8 × 10 inch rectangle. Repeat with the other dough piece. Spread ⅓ of the meringue along one edge of the long side of the shortbread dough. Roll up the rectangle like a jelly roll cake and make sure everything is wrapped in parchment paper. Repeat with the remaining dough and another ⅓ of the meringue. (That part of the preparation is really sticky, but there's no way around it.) Let the rolls sit in the freezer for about 30 minutes. Meantime, preheat the oven to 300°F.

Slice the rolls into ½-inch-thick slices and place them, with a little room between each cookie, on a baking sheet lined with parchment paper. Distribute the rest of the meringue over the cookies.

Bake the cookies in the middle of the oven for about 45 minutes. Let them cool on the tray.

Acknowledgments

I want to give my thanks, with lots of bubbles and fanfare, to all of you without whom I could not have made this book:

Marcus—There is no one else on the planet with whom I'd rather cook, empty vacuum cleaner bags, or share laughs and the future. Without you, damned if there would have been either a good book or a Lisa.

My wonderful family, who always pep me up and support me, drive all over the country, test my food, speak their minds, and inspire. Special thanks to my grandmother Lilly and grandfather Rolf—my ninety-year-old idols!

All the fantastic friends and acquaintances, near and dear, who drop everything when the dinner bell rings, drive untold miles, lend their stuff, houses, and homes, and happily pose for pictures, despite the storm clouds brewing in the background or that someone just had a baby a week earlier! No one named, no one forgotten. You are all wonderful, and I owe all of you a lifetime of amazing dinners.

Åsa Dahlgren—the world's most phenomenal photographer, my partner in crime, and my rock.

There aren't many people who would empty the compost for me . . .

Tobias Ohlson—for being one hell of an assistant!

The master's master, designer Kai Ristilä, who works faster than anyone I've ever met and also does it so incredibly well that one can only be amazed.

Bonnier Fakta: Thanks to all the wonderful people at Sveavägen who always support, encourage, and believe in my crazy ideas. Special thanks *till tidernas* most phenomenal editor Annika Ström, and, certainly not least, the publisher's publisher number one, Kerstin Bergfors.

Stålboms Konditori, I have the key to your cottage, but you have the key to my heart. Thank you for so generously sharing with me!

Ekängen Properties, thank you for letting us have a cocktail party on the parking garage rooftop! Next time, you are all welcome, too!

The most amazing suppliers: Solhaga Stenungsbageri, Ugglarpsgrönt, Fiskmeny Hönö, Gudmundsgården, and Gårdsbutiken Thuressons.

Index

Measurements and Equivalents

Metric Equivalents Liquid*

U.S. quantity	Metric equivalent
¼ teaspoon	1 ml
½ teaspoon	2.5 ml
¾ teaspoon	4 ml
1 teaspoon	5 ml
1¼ teaspoons	6 ml
1½ teaspoons	7.5 ml
1¾ teaspoons	8.5 ml
2 teaspoons	10 ml
1 tablespoon	15 ml
2 tablespoons	30 ml
⅛ cup	30 ml
¼ cup *(2 fluid ounces)*	60 ml
⅓ cup	80 ml
½ cup *(4 fluid ounces)*	120 ml
⅔ cup	160 ml
¾ cup *(6 fluid ounces)*	180 ml
1 cup *(8 fluid ounces)*	240 ml
1½ cups *(12 fluid ounces)*	350 ml
3 cups	700 ml
4 cups *(1 quart)*	950 ml *(.95 liter)*

This chart can also be used for small amounts of dry ingredients, such as salt and baking powder.

Metric Equivalents Dry

Ingredient	1 cup	¾ cup	⅔ cup	½ cup	⅓ cup	¼ cup	2 tbsp
All-purpose gluten-free flour	160g	120g	106g	80g	53g	40g	20g
Granulated sugar	200g	150g	130g	100g	65g	50g	25g
Confectioners' sugar	100g	75g	70g	50g	35g	25g	13g
Brown sugar, firmly packed	180g	135g	120g	90g	60g	45g	23g
Cornmeal	160g	120g	100g	80g	50g	40g	20g
Cornstarch	120g	90g	80g	60g	40g	30g	15g
Shortening	190g	140g	125g	95g	65g	48g	24g
Chopped fruits and vegetables	150g	110g	100g	75g	50g	40g	20g
Chopped seeds	150g	110g	100g	75g	50g	40g	20g
Ground seeds	120g	90g	80g	60g	40g	30g	15g